Love and the Sacred Song of the Hedgerow

Through the seasons, a hedgerow sings its poetry into the life of a man in search of his heart and the infinity of Love.

Alastair R. McNeilage

Copyright © 2024 by Alastair McNeilage. All rights reserved. No portion of this book, except for brief review, may be reproduced, stored in a retrieval system, or transmitted in any form or by any means—electronic, mechanical, photocopying, recording, or otherwise—without the written permission of the author.

All illustrations by Ella McNeilage. Copyright © 2024

Published by Awaytobetogether.com
March 2025

Paperback ISBN 978-1-0684135-0-6
Hardback ISBN 978-1-0684135-1-3

To Chantek

Contents

Acknowledgments   vii
Introduction   xi

Part One

1. Invincible light   9
2. Our sacred nostalgia   20
3. Reverence   32

Part Two

4. Self Love   47
5. The charity of suffering   58
6. Surrender   68

Part Three

7. The Prayer of Beauty   81
8. The loving touch of Attention   90
9. Goodness   102

Part Four

10. Gladness   117
11. The justice of Humility   126
12. The last darkness of Love   136

About the Author   145

Acknowledgments

I offer, as best I can, my deepest gratitude to all the mystics through the ages, across many traditions, who have dared to bear testament to their encounters with a Love that is eternal, infinite and divine. I include among them all the trees in the hedgerow that have sung their songs to my heart as I walked beside them.

Saffron Walden
    March 2025

Glossary

The language of Love is always alive in us. In every spiritual tradition a small number of sacred words - used to intimate the nameless - still carry in them a precious call. They are gatekeepers to the immensity to which we belong. In the midst of our lives, they call us to the light and whisper us back home.

These words do not yield their meaning at first glance: when we meet them, they invite us to journey deeper, through the resonance of our hearts, into their unspoken guidance.

As each word carves an engraving of its testament within us, we bring our own unique language to describe the encounter. I offer, here, a personal reflection of their narrative in my own life.

Charity. To give in reverence for all that is given to us.

Divine. Belonging to our true home in the infinity of Oneness.

Faith. A wordless knowing that holds us fast to the sacred path of our homecoming.

Holy. That which connects us in wholeness to the loving Source of life.

Humility. To be surrendered to the will of Love.

Grace. The knowledge bearer of eternal Love, gifted to all Being.

Love. The Great Giving and the Great Receiving, known through the heart.

Mercy. Everlasting Care for us.

Prayer. A moment of mutuality in love of Being.

Sacred. The manifestation of all that leads us back to eternal Love.

Soul. That in us which already knows of its true home.

When I use these words in the text with a capital letter, they refer to their eternal, boundless nature. When they appear in lower case, they refer to our worldly possession of them.

Introduction

The melody of Love plays through all creation.

Here, in this one precious moment, we are alive. We are "being" and the greatest of all ways of being is Love.

From where I am now, as I cast a glance over my shoulder back to my birth, my childhood and adolescence, my adultness and old age, I can catch the precious moments of my journey through life - both the cries in the dark of all my pain and hurt and, gathered beside them in kindred silence, radiant moments of return when, one mysterious way or another, Love found me.

This journey - the sacrament of our lives - leads us to the mystery and vastness of our human heart and, in the midst of all our confusion and loss, to know more and more about our home in Love. We are forever being called by a boundless Love back to our divinity and the source of our Being.

The unbreakable bond of life and death is the love song of all nature. The yearning for, and movement towards, more and more being is there in all creation. It is the divine signature of our kinship and our aliveness in the eternity held in each moment of becoming.

All life is woven by the infinite reality of Love. Nothing is sepa-

Introduction

rate from this mystical, magical ocean. Love is there in the first blossom of the Blackthorn, opening to the light of longer days and surrendering itself to Life in the innocence of its faith, before even its leaves have come.

For us, too, the distant presence of a Love that is eternal echoes in the intimacy of every act of kindness, in all beauty and joy, and in the exile of each moment of suffering.

The knowledge of the mind is nothing until it becomes, through Love, the wisdom of the heart.

Not far from my home, in the rolling farmland that surrounds us under the vast continent of an East Anglian sky, a hedgerow snakes it way for nearly a quarter of a mile along the North Western edge of a grassy farm track. It is old and wise and full of Love.

Day and night, season by season, sunlight and moonlight paint their gold and silver upon it. As I pass by, it dedicates to me its Winter nakedness and its full flowering of summer, its garlanded Spring and the autumn fire of its deathless passing.

It has my heart!

The sacred stillness of its being in the howling of Winter gales, in the silence of snow, and in the caress of summer sunshine and gentle rain, teaches me how to Be. It calls me home.

Only in the secret stillness of our human heart do we register the immensity and the intimacy of the truth offered to us by nature, not as a fact that can be spoken or a faith that can be granted to another but as a wordless return towards our true selves in the silence of nature's Being.

The courage to pay the price Love demands rests forever in the deep places of our longing. Naked and utterly vulnerable, we must cross the abyss that burns us free of our illusion of separateness and all that protects us.

We exist because Love pours itself into every moment of our becoming. It is the life granted to us in each sacred breath we breathe and is carried in our blood in the rhythm of each heartbeat.

It doesn't really matter what we call it: Sacred Love, Infinite

Introduction

Love, Loving Oneness, everlasting Goodness, even God's Love. With its touch upon us, we are Christed or Buddha'd or Mohammed'd or Krishna'd or simply blessed, into Being. All nouns and all names become living acts of a wordless search in the union of this encounter with our destiny.

Our journey towards the light of this knowing is simple and difficult. The darkness of our wounding stops us from surrendering to the embrace of a loving Presence that is always here and always in search of us.

We have no choice but to face the impediment of our fearfulness. We instinctively move away from pain towards fleeting moments of happiness but to run from our suffering only takes us further and further away from the immutability of the Love we seek and the truth of who we are.

This Love makes precious all our suffering. If we look closely, we are granted a new revelation: it is our loss and broken-heartedness that point us back to the path home. Only in the grace of our healing can we reclaim our loyalty to Love and our own fullness of being, in the midst of this precious life.

In the deep, restorative stillness of nature I can walk in fellowship with the hedgerow. Just for a moment, a Love that is more than I could ever know passes through this human heart and the hedgerow and I are together in a sacred mutuality. A new life!

Part One

Winter

The darkness of Fire.

The deep stillness of Winter awakens the living flame inside us. Winter is not a movement away from life or a hiding but a gathering-in towards the embracing of light and shadow and the dark presence of an eternal fire that lies deep within our own holiness.

In the silence beyond the noise of words and thoughts, that in us which belongs to Love can hear its own longing for home. The courage of Winter beckons us to turn and face in ourselves all that we would rather refuse.

All that hides in fearfulness has to be invited to its own homecoming. We have to dare to trust that the innocent faith we once knew in our young hearts could again animate our lives. All in us that carries the memory of suffering and shrinks away from open-heartedness has to find its healing, and the resurrection of its trust, in the warmth and welcome of our own loving attention.

In the holy adventure of Winter the heart surrenders to this journey of return through the dark. In the stillness behind every movement of nature, Love deeply penetrates all life. It awakens us to a new relationship to our suffering and all suffering, through a rekindled loyalty to Love.

We see that the breath of a mysterious and boundless Care penetrates every atom as the eternal life-force of all creation. Everything is aflame in Love. When we are lit by its light we see beyond sorrow and pain and the illusion of our separateness. We catch sight of a new covenant that beckons us in from the cold to the fire of a sacred communion.

**In our essence, we are not slaves to ourselves,
nor to the world; we are lovers.
Our freedom and accomplishments
are in love, which is another name for perfect
understanding.
In this ability to understand, in this impregnation
of everything that is,
we are one with Spirit that penetrates
everything, and that is also
the breath of the soul.**

Rabindranath Tagore

December

I crunched through a cold and frosty solstice morning. The first sunshine for a few days lit the last of the flame-red bramble leaves, still painting their colour on the black and grey canvas of the hedgerow.

Low over the Winter wheat fields, a pair of Red Kites danced their intimate ballet on the wind. The ground was brick-hard. A female blackbird, pecking at the remaining sloes that still clung to the bare branches of the blackthorn, flew off as I passed, her startled exclamation calling out to the presence of danger to all who listened.

The wind had turned to the North a few days ago and, with the first heavy frosts, the last leaves of the field maple were falling; their final golden flight, cradled on Winter's breath to the new embrace of a dark earth.

I stood and felt the hedgerow's final exhalation into sleep and its submission to the deepest of trusts in a Spring too distant to see.

As the hedgerow comes to rest in its naked slumber, the Holly remains fully-clothed in its dark green crown of thorns and the blood red of its berries. What is she teaching me? As a sister to her sleeping kin, her white wood heart keeps alive an evergreen loyalty to eternal life. An invincible wish for light rises from the darkness of these short days.

Chapter 1
Invincible light

Love is personal. Every single human being, whether consciously or unconsciously, is their own living exploration of Love. It is both what we are and what we seek to rediscover in every moment of our lives.

Our search for Love is born from a flame that burns within us: the eternal flame from which we are all lit. To know that flame - and its timeless desire - begins, like Winter itself, as a movement within.

One simple message reveals itself when we part the sea of words that gathers around every spiritual way: "DO NOT BE AFRAID. YOU ARE LOVED".

* * *

There is no mystery. Somewhere within us we can still feel our faithfulness to this truth. Some part of us in the fathomless deep of the heart, rests forever in the sacred unity of life and knows the living beauty and justice of this radical, transformational birthright.

Love and the Sacred Song of the Hedgerow

When we are alive to this part of us, the truth of life always "rings true" when we hear it. We *recognise* the call of home and, in the same moment, the deep pain of our exile is felt.

As a fugitive to Love, we are lived by this loss and in that lostness we translate the language of Love through the grammar of happiness. Trapped in our sacred bereavement, we cling to the comfort of brief joys.

Each time we lose our grip on happiness, our true heart's longing reveals itself as an eternal desire for the immutable stillness of peace that accompanies the presence of an infinite Love.

* * *

Our dedication to happiness can become an idolatry of all that is finite. It creates an endless dissatisfaction through which we can discover our true longing for something that is infinite and everlasting, calling us from the far distance of the unknown.

Our longing for Love is there behind all our earthly desires. If we are still enough to listen, we come to see that the innocence of our joy holds within it our sacred ancestry in Love.

We have to rediscover this Love for ourselves; its touch upon us. We have to feel for ourselves love's gateway to the divine, to eternity, and we have to journey into the vastness of certain words we are so used to taking for granted: words like forgiveness, mercy, beauty, grace and, especially, the word Love itself.

* * *

Boundless Love is always trying to shape us in its own image; to

Invincible light

return us to what we are. If we look, it is there in the simple beauty of the body's instinctive wish to open and free itself from tension.

That seemingly involuntary movement hides the divine poetry of a body that can lead us beyond the limits of its own boundary to a new receptivity and a new listening in the symphony of an imminent and immutable Care for us.

* * *

Divine Love flows into our lives in the dark. Most of our actions and our search for a fullness-of-being happen without our being conscious of the wisdom we carry. Only the grace of a deep humility allows us to receive that which is always being offered but which we can never possess. We are not entitled to "have" love: We can only Be Love.

Our movement towards Love requires a sacrifice; an offering up of all in us that would mould life into the shape of our own self-defined happiness. Instead, it is our sorrow that calls Love to light our journey and reveal our deepest self.

Our relationship to Love takes us from the everyday and the personal to the eternity of the infinite - the two worlds to which we are inextricably linked and which can unite within us.

* * *

When we unmask the values of our societies and move away from the victories and the defeats of a competitive world, we begin to embrace the deep knowing of the sacred life within and we become less lonely and more loving. The humility of loving kindness and compassion begins to flow through our makeshift struggle for success and bears us away from all that we do towards the new liberty of our being.

Love and the Sacred Song of the Hedgerow

This - before us now - is the most wonderful journey any human being can make. It requires more bravery and determination than any expedition to the highest mountains or the deepest seas, to the unexplored jungles and remote deserts of the Earth, or to any of the galaxies beyond our world.

* * *

The movement inwards to know ourself more deeply, more consciously and more compassionately, points us towards the true destiny that awaits us all, beyond all the geography we are drawn to and all the peak experiences we chase.

When I agree to this journey and turn towards Love, I find standing there in front of me the greatest of all obstacles - my fear of all that remains unknown, yet without Love's embrace we will always be afraid.

* * *

Our drive for the affirmation of success, of power and status; our frequent retreat away from the world into places of more safety; the comfort of another piece of cake, the physiology of an adrenalin high or the anguished numbing from pain in addiction and harmful behaviours: each of these bids to escape our emptiness holds within them the invincible light of an unspoken longing for an eternal home that lies beyond the cartography of our everyday lives.

We have to cross the great divide to find again what is closer than our own breath. Until then, in the awful illusion of our separateness, we invent an authority and a right to harness the planet's abundance, power and riches for our own gain. We have to vanquish the fearfulness that seeks to manage and control and carve the world around us into the shape we need it

Invincible light

to be, and, instead, allow our lives to be shaped by nature's loving grace.

* * *

Our fear has us dam and dig, cut and burn, buy and sell, profit and possess and force our agenda upon the world around us; and it is faith that bids our hearts turn towards the stillness of nature
and listen deeply.

In the company of the hedgerow, I can feel again the intimacy of life's rhythms. I see how its spirit responds in harmony and balance, through the unchanging innocence of its own being, to the evolving life of the planet and the choreography of each day and each season.

In the silence and the reverence of watching, I am shown how life yields to death and how death, in a sacred reciprocity, gives way to new life and new meaning, far beyond the narrow boundaries of a materialistic and fearful world.

* * *

The odyssey that confronts us is the journey from the head to the heart. It can be the longest journey of them all. It may take a whole lifetime or it can happen in a second. It is a life-changing shift from one way of being in the world to another; from fear to faith, from doing to being, from the contraction of all our defences to the expansive beauty and trust in the true meaning
of our own vulnerability.

We are shown, too, that the deepest impulse of a heart in love is to serve, to give itself away. The sculpted salt image of our ego that protects us in life secretly longs to be dissolved again by the sea and become once more a servant to the will of the ocean's embrace.

Love and the Sacred Song of the Hedgerow

* * *

In the realm of the sacred and the eternal there is only ever the deepest of welcomes. All in nature moves and is loved for its journey of purpose and beauty. Until I join in that holiest of communions, I am lived by the dark spell of a sacred wound - a memory of my infant hurt and all the loneliness, shame and trembling that accompanied my first experience of feeling lost to an all-sustaining Love.

The ancient magic of nature that dances in the hedgerow can weave us back into the fabric of the universe. In the unity of all we receive we can live a shared meaning that allows our joy in life to benefit humankind and all creation.

All that unifies us in the Oneness of life becomes divine through the awakening of the human heart. We come to see that our return to innocence allows us to know Love again and to surrender our obedience to its will.

* * *

The wordless pain and sorrow I carry deeply within me, the scars of all my loss and wounding, is the darkness upon which a new light must shine. It is a darkness that exists in the name of Love.

All my hurts are sacred places, banished by my turning away from what is most painful. The test of my loyalty to a yet unknown Love lies in my willingness to face that in me which has retreated in trepidation from the very thing it longs for the most.

* * *

It is here in our compassionate holding of these abandoned parts of us that we rediscover our original wish to return to the oneness of

Invincible light

connection and belonging. Our longing for eternal Love in all its magnitude, constancy and boundless forgiveness, threads its gold through each moment of our healing journey.

The loyalty of our hearts once again claims its right to bring to our wounding all the qualities of love that were driven away by each painful experience of separateness we endured. We no longer agree to our shame.

We welcome home the prodigality of our heart-brokenness and, in the tenderness of that welcoming, we are bathed again in the healing light of a Truth we once knew. We see that the infinity of true Love is not something we attain; it reveals itself as what we are. In that moment we are holy again.

The path towards this begins with the blessing and the courage of a heart that follows the invincible light of its longing and dares to turn towards the sacred gateway of our suffering.

**The mind creates the abyss.
The heart crosses it.**

Nisagardatta

January

The mood of the afternoon sky darkened with rain clouds from the East as I reached the end of my walk. The light began to fade. The hedgerow was full of pale browns and greys turning black in the cold, wet skeleton of its sleep.

Next to me, a patch of green Poet's Ivy offered me its midwinter worship of life in its own evergreen fullness. To one side of it, I caught the shy colours of lichen in the beauty of its withered shapes and hollows, feeding on the bare, spiky branches of a hawthorn. You had to look closely to catch the brightness of reds, yellows, whites and pale greens, painted in secret over black bark under the grey of an overcast sky.

All at once, the wind dropped. I could feel a stillness descend like the quiet of snow. I stopped and allowed the sudden silence of not moving to gather around me. All the noise of my life gave way to dusk.

The Ivy stood guard in the twilight, a solitary prophet to the gathering of all four seasons. Its faith is woven through the hedgerow as a deathless promise of new life to its brothers and sisters who wait in the dark dream of Winter.

The stillness and intimacy of this new year have yet to grant access to the rhythm of Spring and the spreading of wild garlands through the church of these trees and plants. Like them, all that I am is still held in the distance of a sacred memory, waiting to awaken.

Chapter 2
Our sacred nostalgia

Love is the light calling us home. It holds us captive. Every dimension of our lives is governed by our relationship to Love. The further we are from that eternal home, the more we know what it is to suffer. We enter life in the splendour of our helplessness and purity, bringing with us, as we come, a sacred memory of connection to an oceanic Love that is boundless and everlasting.

From the moment of our birth until our last breath, we carry into life our hidden longing for this home. Whatever suffering we meet in life, our lostness to the infinity of Love is the one wound we all share as both the illusion and the truth of our lives. Until we entered this world, we had no understanding of separateness.

* * *

Alongside this subtle exile, we can still remember moments of freedom and closeness; feeling steady and sure in the love of those who opened their hearts to us. We can still touch the child's thrill of

Our sacred nostalgia

new discoveries and moments of wonder when our innocence and delight carried our parents deeper into beauty and the heart of things.

However carefree and happy our childhood, our gossamer sensitivity registered (and still registers), more deeply than we know, the slightest disconnection from all that is loving. Without a sense of that connection we are unable to trust in this new world.

If we lose the truth of being loved, fear becomes the shadowed testament of our lives. We must journey to rediscover the hidden meaning of our own pain in order to walk free again in the certainty of our hearts. Until then we are lost in our own innocent betrayal.

* * *

With no intention behind it, the deepest of all our earthly wounds begins with those who love us. As pure infant beings, still close to our timeless birthright, we look for the oceanic embrace of our own preciousness in the faces of those around us.

Instead, lost to the origin of their own lives, those who care for us express a love that is no longer conscious of its infinite source. In the depth of our still-sacred cry we encounter from them a finite love, uncertain of its ancestry; a love that can be withdrawn.

When those brief but devastating moments come, all in us that wished to surrender in awe to the beauty and joy of Love is plunged into the darkness of a wordless doubt about our welcome and our worth.

* * *

We are pierced by the same unintentional teaching that was forced upon every generation before us when they first journeyed into life -

Love and the Sacred Song of the Hedgerow

that the love we can expect is conditional upon our behaviour and governed by the psychological life of our parents. Navigating the drama of that uncertainty consumes the rest of our lives.

The sacred, loving infinity we waited to envelope us is usurped by a love subject to the illusion of separateness, emanating from the heart-wounds of our family and the conditions into which we are born.

As the divine abundance we knew recedes into our still-fresh past, we discover the loneliness of exile from a reality that, just a short time ago, had embraced us in the infinity of a limitless Love.

We fall from the light, carrying our sacred wisdom into the dark, hidden sanctuary of our uncertain hearts. In its place, we are caught in the memory of a betrayal that makes us fearful of initiating our own movement towards love. In the innocence of our young awareness, we carry into our lives an unseen dread and a doubt in our own goodness.

We feel separate. We hide parts of us in shame. In our helplessness, as emanations of one Light and one Love and one Will, we fall further and further from the sacred. Slowly, we become less and less open to the whispered confessional of Love's beauty, generosity and care in each flower and each sunrise and each crystal wave of light upon the sea of all we witness in our lives.

In this banishment, we have no choice but to will into the world a version of ourselves that we are taught best attracts a taste of that Love we no longer sense as freely offered. We go in search of

Our sacred nostalgia

happiness, affirmation and the approval of others from behind a carefully crafted mask.

* * *

These distant cousins of Love offer us brief moments of remembrance that touch us back into relationship - however briefly - to some far-off, echoed feeling of the limitless Love and connection we once knew. We learn to swim in the waters of our young lives while, hidden in our secret wounding, a part of us is still in search of the ocean.

Through the gift of Grace, all that is divine can lift the veil of our blindness at any moment. Suddenly, we stop trying to live life on our terms and accept, instead, the gentle command of a will, beyond the finiteness of our own, that grants us access to our true destiny.

* * *

Our lostness to the infinitely-loving source of our being remains the deepest cause of our suffering. We are caught in an invincible dissatisfaction that is constantly disappointed by a happiness that is only ever fleeting.

We live our lives in a constant state of want as we search for the next good feeling in all that is available to us. Nothing finite can satisfy our longing for the infinite and so we are constantly trapped in our wish for 'more'; a wish mercilessly exploited by all those in search of worldly power.

* * *

Our holy desire now masquerades itself as a need to feel the fulness of more money , more success, more possessions, more pleasure, more

Love and the Sacred Song of the Hedgerow

satisfaction and more spirituality. We dedicate all our time and energy to these things because, for a moment, they awaken a feeling in us that is distantly reminiscent of how it felt when we were One with our source, in Love.

The inevitable failure of our competitive striving plunges us into the wordless dread of being visited again by the pain of believing in our unloveableness and so often our courage fails us, yet we can never escape our secret wish for an enduring Love. We carry forever an intuition of all that is sacred in the subtle memory of our true self. Love is always calling us to the divinity of our Oneness.

* * *

All human behaviour and all suffering has behind it this sacred nostalgia. The purity of our buried knowledge of divine Love lies, as our innermost longing and secret desire, behind every experience of pain and failure and behind every action we take in our lives.

We are constantly called home, yet we do not hear: it is hard to pull ourselves free from the magnetic force of daily life and allow all of ourselves to be open and vulnerable in front of the unknown.

* * *

Giving away our hearts is not easy when we defend against the risk of new hurt and betrayal. In that ever-alert vigilance we remain forever sensitive to the slightest brush of an unloving look.

The hidden burden of our forsakenness weighs upon our shoulders. We find confirmation for our defences in the changeable behaviour of all those whose own hearts have been equally bruised, and we retreat back again into the safety of our self-imposed hiding.

Our sacred nostalgia

* * *

We cannot wish this wound away. It belongs to our loyalty to Love and carries a scar that only the light of our own love can heal. It is the story of our deepest self and forms the precious vulnerability and wholeness through which we can claim our kindredness and loving connection to the human family.

Only our own intentional open-heartedness can begin to bring to the exiled places in us all that they have always wanted - loving kindness, compassionate understanding and the deep, unconditional warmth of welcome and acceptance.

This new touch of our self-love - the incarnate emissary of the infinite Love to which we belong - gathers us back and begins to dissolve the illusion of our separateness and the deep-seated belief that we are alone in our suffering.

* * *

In this compassionate opening towards myself, all my contraction recedes and my awareness of the divine Love to which I belong can finally gain a foothold.

As we meet ourselves with this deeper acceptance, we become more receptive to the greater Love that embraces us and the wounded bearer of our secret longing, until now concealed from the world, is welcomed as the richness of who we are.

* * *

If I do not accept the unbreakable bond between my joys and my sorrows, my suffering remains cast out in the darkness and, in this state of solitariness, I cannot fully open to the healing light of Love.

Love and the Sacred Song of the Hedgerow

My wish to turn away from the brokenness of the heart fragments me from my wholeness. Only the gentle warmth of loving attention cradles, the richness of my being, the secret wisdom of my forgotten home.

Whatever season I carry within me, the hedgerow bears my secrets in its branches. In the stillness of its life, I am shown again the pain and the joy of faith.

* * *

Slowly, in praise of a new holiness, my eyes are opened. I come to see that we are all deeply connected and that we are all loved. We are brought into being in every moment of our lives by the limitless, loving force of life. It is a truth that can be seen in all nature when we drop ever deeper into the intimacy of the present moment. Here, now, the gospel of our lives in all its joy, and the sorrow of our lostness, are bound together in a sacred alliance.

As we open towards ourselves, we grant access to the holiness of all that is tender, kind and compassionate and allow its healing to fall upon our loneliness: we are found again in the divinity of a greater Love.

* * *

All that I wish for myself, as a new year begins, has its root in my longing for happiness, fulfilment and peace. All the things I decide that might make me happy will come and go but the deepest wish behind all my desire belongs to eternity and to the prodigal return to a home that binds us all to the common humanity of our broken and bruised hearts.

* * *

Our sacred nostalgia

In the depth of this connection we are held in infinite Love; we are celebrated and seen in infinite forgiveness and respect for all the wrong-doing and suffering that comes out of our lostness to Love.

We touch again the threshold of healing and a new birth in our wholeness. Our faith in the truth of Love comes alive within us and, as we hold our neighbour in the look of a new understanding, the light of our own self-compassion shines brightly upon the darkness of all human suffering.

**We do not need to go out
And find love;
rather, we need to be still
and let love discover us"**

John O'Donohue

February

The ground, which had been frosted hard, is now sodden and wet after days of rain carried in on a stubborn north-westerly. It is still cold but I can just feel the presence of a new force beginning to awaken. The hedgerow stirs to a distant beat that begins to sound out of the stillness of Winter. A congregation of waking faces lift towards the light.

The snowdrops are out, catkins grow yellow on the hazels and bring with them the secrets of inspiration and fertility. The magical Hazel, the faithful herald of hope, is the first to break free from the brittle grip of ice. It murmurs the soft greeting of a different season.

Today has brought the welcome of blue sky and a sun that began to hold some warmth in it. I could feel its touch gently begin to coax open the cells of my body. But February is fickle. In the late afternoon, after darkness fell, a bitter wind veered further to the North and hurled sleet against the exposed flank of the hedgerow, lest I forget that winter is not yet willing to abdicate its throne.

The breaking of the following dawn, though, brought other gifts. I heard the sacred music of early morning bird song for the first time this year and my heart leapt in gratitude and joy. In the same moment the dark sorrow of another season passing sewed the bright thread of time through the pastel cloth of all that is yet to come.

The hedgerow, in the nobility of its prayer, refuses nothing. While some of its dead still hang from its branches, It holds fast to the wisdom of harmony and beauty in the new life that is waiting. What in me remains fearful of death and yet longs for the freedom of the hazel's deep, reverential acceptance? Where is my own Amen, my "so be it"?

Chapter 3
Reverence

Love is reverence. The divinity of the infinite is bound into our lives. Love is pouring itself into us in every sacred moment of life. We recognise its touch upon us when the timeless ocean of its loving Presence gathers around our suffering and we are filled by Love's reverence for itself.

Boundless Love is always in search of us but we are lost to its light in the blindness and contraction of our deepest hurt.

The illusion of our unworthiness is the invisible wound we carry with us in all our turnings towards love. It insists upon its fear of another rejection taking precedence over our longing. Instead of bringing us together, it can leave us lonely and hesitant as we move out in search of each other.

Instead of turning inwards to bring welcome and understanding to ourselves, we go looking for love through the approval and affirmation

Reverence

of others. It is only when all that we withhold from sight inevitably comes into view that the sacred gateway of suffering first appears as a crisis of confusion and distress.

* * *

How do I allow the infinite Care of Love to help me face the finiteness of my own suffering? How do I allow the tender kindness of my own loving welcome to penetrate and heal those parts of me that are still distrustful, alone and holding tightly to the memory of an unloveableness that was never true?

We must know Love for ourselves, in ourselves, as ourselves. We must make love personal and intimate, in order to awaken this new quest to know ourselves more deeply.

We find the unexpected doorway to the hidden truth of our lives when we turn towards all that we hide from others, not as something to be destroyed forever but as a lost part of ourselves yet to know the soft touch of our loving attention.

* * *

The hidden treasure of our sorrow offers us a path home to a truth buried in our hearts - that there is another Love infinitely greater than the finiteness of all that defines our daily lives; a Love that is willing to wait for all eternity to embrace us when we finally dare to kneel before it in the reverence of our humility and loyalty.

* * *

We come to discover, in the final deliverance of all our striving for finite worldly happiness, that only the infinite will do.

Love and the Sacred Song of the Hedgerow

Our faith and our trust in Love begin to appear in the midst of our suffering and we no longer need to exploit worldly happiness as a means to banish all we dare not face. We see, instead, the invincible flame of Love sustaining us in the midst of our wounding. Darkness surrenders itself to the light.

* * *

The more we look, the more the pain and confusion of our ego point us towards the preciousness of our humanity, and the humility of our undefended hearts can burn again as the brightest lantern of the one Light. We find ourselves guided by that place of immortal wisdom that rests within us and unites us to all other human beings; a place we call 'the soul'.

Reclaiming our faith in divine Love brings with it a wonderful healing and wholeness to our lives and a willingness to risk being loved in all our vulnerability. All in us that is restless and dissatisfied finally discovers the gentle might of a new kind of peace.

* * *

Love lies there, waiting, behind our wounding and distress, behind the violence we witness, behind our lostness and behind all our strategies and defences. All it needs to gain entry into our lives and sustain us through our suffering is the bidding of our reverence.

We must dare to believe in Love again. The luminosity of the truth has to be whispered back to shine in our lives once more, even as it re-awakens ancient fears.

Deep within us, we will always carry the dread memory of our exile when we last allowed the innocence of our longing to break free in all its fulness of need.

Reverence

This inheritance is the greatest of all the obstacles we face. The shock of conditionality and limitation that accompanied our first experience of finite, worldly love continues to distance us from the deepest feelings of the divine communion to which we belong.

* * *

The darkness of this loss still flows through the bloodline of ancestral wounding, unintentionally visited upon us by even the most loving of parents.

In the very early months of life, we are at our most sensitive to the presence or the absence of contact. When our search for all that is loving is not reflected back from the face of care-givers who are stressed, anxious or fearful, we are plunged into the lostness of disconnection.

* * *

Without the bandwidth of awareness to understand what is happening in the psychological world of those around us, we can find ourselves imprisoned by the solitary grip of self-shame and fear.

Now, a voice, so familiar we think of it as our own, carries into our adulthood and whispers its protective warning into our ears each time we seek to move out into the world of others. Its dread words force our retreat: "You're not good enough"; "You won't be wanted. You won't be welcome".

We find ourselves lowering our heads, forever lost to our fullness. Somehow, though, buried deep in that brokenness, the far-off sound of the ocean to which we once belonged still haunts the way we live and we bravely move towards relationship.

Love and the Sacred Song of the Hedgerow

* * *

When we turn to face the anguish, pain and tragedy of our feeling-of-being-separate, we find the half-heard voice of our longing for an enduring and boundless Love, calling us back towards our wholeness and guiding the very purpose of our existence on Earth.

To hear that voice and find that purpose, we first have to overcome our fear of Love, held in the shame of our banishment: this scar is branded into the delicate skin of our hearts as a trepidation that often bars our way.

* * *

To risk loving another is a reverence towards ourselves. As we come to know the grace and the courage to believe in the divinity of Love, we unveil the compassion and the loving understanding to meet our own wounding, and the wounding of others, and dissolve the isolation and shame in which it is so often held. The luminosity of our innocence and our faith is restored to us.

Our newly-awakened loyalty to the divinity of all that is whole refuses to allow our wounds to define who we are. Instead, we can hold dear the one who suffers behind the suffering itself - the keeper of the immortal flame within us that seeks the infinity to which we belong and the truth that we - and all nature - are loved into being.

* * *

Gradually, from this day onwards, we begin to reveal our long-forgotten fidelity to the holiness of our Being. We can rest lightly in the ground of our body that continues to show its own loyalty to this Life both in the protective safety of its contraction and in its willingness to surrender.

Reverence

The light is beginning to grow and the days are getting longer. The tender push of the hedgerow towards wakefulness welcomes my own carefully-guarded vulnerability. The quiet power of infant innocence proclaims the courage to believe in all that I long for.

* * *

As a flower yields itself to the morning sun, the heart shows its reverence by softening and opening to the divinity of connection. Our heads lift up, our chests let go their tightness; our hearts open and become more trusting in the presence of an infinitely loving Care that pours itself into us without conditions.

In response, the mind, too, opens into the deep inner space of new understanding and clarity as the touch of the heart's loving acceptance gently offers all that is fearful and alone its way home.

* * *

It is through this redemptive embrace that it becomes possible to fully be with our wounding. We are no longer lived by fear and we refuse to turn away from all that our pain reveals. In these moments (however often they might come and go) the heart, mind and body are willing to be deeply affected by a true understanding of our suffering and its intimate relationship to divine Love.

When this happens we can, at last, see the longing behind all our worldly ways and the loyalty of self-serving strategies that, until now, have forced their limit upon our lives. However powerful those strategies are and however thick their veil of blindness, they are ultimately energised by a wish for peace and a longing to believe in that one single truth that can reach us in our new and grounded vulnerability - "I am loved".

Love and the Sacred Song of the Hedgerow

* * *

As new pilgrims on the path, we can offer our wounding what it has never known - the warmth, understanding and kindness of a love that can at last dissolve being-shame and liberate us from the imprisoning life-statements that gather around the illusion of our own unloveableness.

Over time, this transformation can grant us freedom and rid us of a tyranny that has governed our lives and robbed us of an aliveness that wishes nothing more than to joyfully sing its praise of Being.

* * *

Turning to face what we fear most in ourselves is a reverential moment. We become believers again, disciples of the Love we seek. In time, all those hidden feelings held in the lostness of fear, anger, shame and grief are finally offered the loving, listening benevolence our witnessing.

* * *

In the midst of this profound surrender, our wholeness is able, once again, to take its true place in the world through the rapture and fullness of our own unique song.

The hedgerow never fails to call me home. It - like us - already belongs to the destination we seek to reach - not as a geography, nor a biology but as a faithful commemoration of the enduring peace to be found in the sanctity of Oneness.

Our reverence for the healing journey of our lives, expressed through our body, heart and mind, points the exiled, wounded places in us

Reverence

back towards their true home in the holiness of unity to which we belong.

*** * ***

As I examine more deeply within myself the true meaning of my life, there is revealed a dance between the prose of my existence and the poetry of my Being in which all my wounding is exposed as a lostness to the divinity of Love. In acknowledging this lostness, I am found.

Our journey home is seeded by a love for ourselves that has no choice but to flower into a love for our neighbour. There is no agenda of "my own" in this movement towards the holiness of all that is implied by the word 'together'.

The sacred mutuality of suffering binds us all in its fellowship. Through this love, we meet with one another in a living reverence for all that we are.

Part Two

Spring

The lightness of Being.

The force of Love, animating all life, becomes more visible now as the awakening heart of the hedgerow pours out the sweet-scented blossom of its obedience. We, too, bound to the same heart, feel this movement towards the light. In the shared grace of a new season, something in us wakes to the joy of rebirth.

What was lost is found again, not as a possession but as the gift of our sacrifice and humility to all that offers us its grace. We are here, as incarnate life, to witness the flow of Being and the passage of Love between us and through us into the oneness and embrace of all we see.

Our longing is Love's longing for itself. The tender bud of innocence flowers into our holiness, as we rejoice in the beatitude of a new day and the blessedness of each moment.

A new sun reaches higher in our sky. We shine brighter. The fire of Love begins to refine us as the warmth of loving awareness enters to allow our very vulnerability to strengthen our faith. We begin to take our place in the world in the alchemy of a new humility.

As each season gently surrenders to the next so we approach our brokenness through the compassion of a deeper understanding. The soft spring rain of an unspoken joy melts the cold of our sorrow, and the lost covenant of all that remains caught in the illusion of being alone is revealed in the mercy of our own remorse.

**Start with your peace, your love, your compassion
and go from there.
And then love everything…everything.
Let's all walk each other home.**

Ram Dass

March

I was out early in the cold of a March dawn. By the time I had covered the two miles across the fields to the hedgerow, its bare bones were being painted in the bright gold of a sunrise. Dewdrops, dangling from the smallest branches, blazed in fire.

In the hedgerow, the first awakening and blessing of Spring gathered itself around the courage of the Elder. Its new leaves, always the first to show, open like hands raised in prayer. They sound the clarion call of their joy to beckon others from the deep of their Winter sanctuary into the light of a new season.

This spirit tree writes the genesis of its first leafing into the chronicles of Spring, as it holds fast to its faithfulness in a season yet to reveal itself fully. The bright loyalty of its young leaves offers me its lesson in vulnerability and strength. They call me to trust in my own open-heartedness; to allow my own faith in all that cannot be known and to let the unpredictability of March winds brush against my innocence without any certainty of their kindness.

Somehow the hedgerow, through each changing season, graces me its example of fragility and invincible will. The Elder, which flowers, fruits and withers back to its loyal rest, submits itself to an eternal cycle that is never broken. In that surrender, it flies free from its own boundary into the wisdom of Love.

By the afternoon, the warmth of the sun had begun to spread its touch upon the land. The cold receded, just as my own fears dare to give way to hope in the fathomless abyss of Love's inexhaustible mercy.

Chapter 4
Self Love

Love is the joy of its own blessing. Everything is penetrated by Love. Everything existing sings the love of its own being. When everything is stripped back to the first impulse of its arising, Love is there. If we can slowly but surely allow ourselves to be lived by this reality, everything changes.

We come to know Love as the infinite reality, there in the turning towards all our relationships - to ourselves, to all others and to the world around us. In the midst of each meeting we discover our selves.

All by which we judge ourselves and others as separate is transformed into the compassion and mercy of a loving witness bound in kindred fidelity to Love. We become One.

* * *

Our faithfulness to Love begins to grow when we dare to become more loving towards ourselves. We cannot offer the wholeness of our loving acceptance to those around us, or fully open to the infinity of a

Love and the Sacred Song of the Hedgerow

loving Presence, until we bring that same loving relationship to all that has become fragmented within ourselves. Without that, we remain too contracted to receive new truths and, inevitably, we continue to judge in others all that we still refuse to face and understand in ourselves.

Only when we allow the divine qualities of Love to flow in us are they free to pass unhindered towards those around us. It is through the truth of loving kindness, compassion, joyfulness-of-being and the music of stillness, resounding in the stillness of our hearts, that we begin to live the power and beauty of our destiny and to feel called to the depths of that most sacred of words - "together".

* * *

To rest in the heart is to allow a new loyalty to Love to take precedence over our fear. We accept ourselves in the whole-heartedness of who we are without having to defend or hide the wound entombed in the love-story of our lives.

Love is always pressing its embrace upon all who suffer. All in me that was hidden from sight is revealed as my estrangement from all that is true. I begin to allow the love-language of the heart to lay bare all my joys and sorrows and fears.

* * *

It is faith in my own healing that gives compassion free passage to dissolve the contraction of my judgement and reactivity and allows me to enter the warmth of a new understanding of others.

It is then that our hearts reveal their true beauty in the miracle of a new meeting. When we rest in the holiness of understanding and

Self Love

forgiveness, the loving awareness in which we are held extends its touch towards others and we live our lives in testimony to the Light.

* * *

Offering our care and open-heartedness to the world breaks us free. The root of all our vulnerability - the loss of our faith in Love - is the kindred wound each of us carries. We know the deepest signature of our warm-heartedness when we see our pain expressing itself in the lives of others.

Equally, when they witness their tears and fearfulness in us, a natural flow of compassion and loving kindness arises. Each of us can touch what the other is feeling. In this sacred mutuality and reciprocity we see the true nature of harmony in the presence of a divine Will that penetrates all our lives in our pilgrimage towards Love.

The blessing of Love that has gathered around our own wounding, commands us to represent into life that same blessing towards others.

* * *

Now the true sacrifice demanded of us is revealed. We stand in humility at the gateway to a new world when we are able to say *"I love and am loved"*. To believe in Love - even if it resides in our hope and faith - surrenders us to a universal beauty and mercy, which can only appear in relationship.

* * *

In the quiet of our faith, all our doing becomes the sacred poetry of the one Will and the meaning and purpose of our lives finally expresses itself in the benediction of our becoming.

Love and the Sacred Song of the Hedgerow

We move from the confinement of our own created sufferings to the sacred mutuality of all suffering. This is the holiness of our journey back from the head to the heart, towards a loving, eternal embrace that awaits us and sustains us as we walk ourselves, and each other, home.

* * *

It sounds simple but it is not easy. I am the skilled impersonator of my own wounding. Behind all the strategies, defences and reactivity of the wonderful, inventive personality, there lies the shadow of all fear. Each threat of judgement casts us adrift and our openness and innocence are overwhelmed by the dread of rejection.

Yet something calls. The deep whisper of a hidden faith still echos our hidden fidelity to Love. The sound of the Ocean still carry its tides within us.

* * *

Later, when that fidelity turns our awareness to face our fear, we meet a child's broken-heartedness.
Safety lies in keeping away from my most painful feelings. This child of mine, burdened by hidden shame and the constant fear of not being welcome, is forever trapped in the drama and inconsistencies of human love.

* * *

I walk through an ancestral hall of mirrors that distorts the shape of my life. I no longer believe in myself and my own worth. I succumb to a fear of my own nakedness, carved into my growing heart by the refusal of all that I longed for.

Self Love

How, then, do I learn to trust that which I believe betrayed me? Our first tentative step is to drop more deeply into the dark beauty of our hearts. There we will discover, buried beyond sight, a knowing that contradicts a belief in our loneliness and shame and beckons us, instead, towards the freedom of loving ourselves and others in the bond of a common destiny.

In the transformation of this more compassionate relationship to ourselves, we come to see that suffering belongs to us all and when we allow those divine qualities of Love to touch our own inner life, they begin to flow towards others. Through our actions and our Being, we can belong again to the loving source of all creation.

The grace of a deeper, more loving acceptance towards myself brings with it a new faith in life. I begin to see how life can say "yes!" to me and I become less fearful of acknowledging my own need and more open to the call of what life wants from me.

Greater access to the all-seeing eye of the heart allows me to pause and become more open to all each day has to offer. I become less afraid to meet life in a new way. I begin to trust and rejoice in its benevolence and justice.

I come to see that my preciousness lies hidden in my pain and suffering. All in me that knows of isolation and loneliness begins to feel the wish to know Love in the joyful company of others.

My defences and fears are gently dissolved by the touch of my own

Love and the Sacred Song of the Hedgerow

kindness and understanding. As I soften and risk owning my vulnerability, I become more permeable to the infinite Care that waits patiently to enter my awareness and become known.

* * *

Seeing the world as Love can only take place in the heart. The mind knows consciousness, the body knows the harmony of beauty but only the deep sanctuary at the heart of the soul can know everything as Love.

We return to the light to reclaim our faith in the loving oneness and mercy of the life we are given in every moment. All that we trusted in the innocence of our young hearts we now know to be true. We can belong again, in the joy of our being, to the grandeur of unconditional everlasting Love, there in the mercy of all that is creative.

A living faith dares us to be more loving, to slowly begin to liberate ourselves from a life of fear and contraction. We become more reachable and more openly receptive to all that is given. We accept ourselves as ancient believers in life's benediction. The Grace of all we receive has brought us home.

* * *

Now we can place our lives on the great potter's wheel of our experience and gently shape them into vessels with more and more capacity to be filled by Love.

The power of nature awakens us again and again to this deepest sense of connection to all life and in that 'all' we find a loving awareness that is always in search of us.

It is in this moment that I am beckoned in from the cold to take my

Self Love

place by the fire of friendship and community, and those already there welcome me in to the kinship of a suffering and a joy that binds us all to its sacred meaning.

Love, through its emissaries of loving kindness, compassion, joyfulness and the divine stillness of mercy, flows through all that still lives in the hollowness of isolation and, in the deep of sacred silence, awakens it to the power of our own love in the unity of Oneness.

**When you step back from stressing the parts,
when the mind becomes still,
the rose comes to you,
unfolds in you in all its glory.
The perfume invades you completely.
The rose is you.
You are one.**

Jean Klein

April

There was a frost two days ago as another rain front spiralled down from the north and left behind it a clear, cold night sky.

Today, the rain is back pounding the land, turning its indentations into grassy bogs. Deep pools of brown water fill the hollows where tractor wheels have sunk their treads deep into the clay. Even the shallow ditch under the hedgerow is full to the brim.

Water pours down the track as it bends around two ancient oaks and then turns more to the South before descending through a sodden field of Winter wheat to a footbridge over a deep gully where a roaring stream is almost hidden by overhanging hazels.

The Blackthorn, dark mother and keeper of secrets and the tarot of the hedgerow's fate, long since laid bare the beauty of her star-white blossom. Now, unconcealed, she waits for her newly-birthed leaves to once again clothe her in flowing garments of bright green.

In the wet, she is brazen, fierce and stern-eyed. Whether she is naked or adorned in the brightness of Spring, she holds no truck with shame or guilt.

The white spindrift of her blossom has nearly gone; either blown free by early April gales or battered to the ground by this heavy rain. It doesn't matter to her. Her thoroughbred dignity remains. She is revealed in the silence of her defiance, as the pure chalice of the hedgerow's soul, helpless before the irresistible call of Love.

I can feel the echo of her faith in me.

Chapter 5
The charity of suffering

Love is the wordless voice of all giving. Life abandons itself into the limitless generosity of the divine, from which springs the eternal longing in us to give ourselves to the Love that is always giving itself to us. We recognise ourselves as Love.

This sacred reciprocity flows through all existence. The extent to which I am able to embrace it and join in the dance of its giving and receiving depends upon my ability to offer up my suffering and all my defences to the presence of an all-loving and eternal embrace.

When we feel this connection, its presence begins to spread within us, just as the grip of winter darkness recedes and the days themselves grow towards the light. We begin to see the world of our everyday activity through this Light in the simplicity of love and faith and in the gentle, joyful spontaneity of a sacred abundance. We belong again to wholeness.

* * *

The charity of suffering

Here, in the deepest womb of Silence, life gives itself to its own birthing and awakens the soul to its secret lineage.

It is then that the sacred sweetness of Charity pours itself through us and out towards others; and in each of these moments when the heart gives of itself, it becomes more divine.

When Silence becomes known, its deepest knowledge, its revelation to us all, is: "You are loved". Allowing the flow of that truth to pass through us and radiate out towards all things is the path of each sacred Way.

Our captive hearts long to open to the beauty and preciousness of life so that they can be swept up in the freedom and joy of waking to the Spring of each new day.

A heart surrendered to Love allows this music to play through us, not as something we can command but as an irresistible light shining in such a way that the blindness of seeing all things as separate is swept away.

We are the living remembrance of the ocean, held in the light of Love, in which the giver and the receiver are one. Now, we can know Love as the holiness of Charity giving itself away across all eternity.

Our hearts carry the chalice of this secret behind all our sorrow. When our innermost desire is met by the grace of loving consciousness, knowledge transforms into wisdom, and kindness gathers around our suffering and the suffering of others.

Love and the Sacred Song of the Hedgerow

We sing the praise of Love when silence stills our hearts and our desire to possess transmutes from 'mine' into the sacred name of service.

* * *

This inexhaustible flow of charity presses itself upon us as a limitless, loving giving, and all the while I stand, alone, in a search for freedom that has become disguised as a journey to be free of suffering: I persist in looking for happiness in the fleetingness of all that comes and goes.

In this, I am confronted by the dread reality that nothing in my worldly life lasts. It is death, in all its ruthless loyalty to the truth, that brings us precious moments of humility when we discover again, in the spectre of loss, a heightened receptivity to Life and to the living current of Love flowing between us.

In the midst of all the noise and drama of life, the experience of being loved, affirmed, celebrated, fulfilled and met in the safety of loving kindness writes upon our hearts the directions of the "home" we seek.

* * *

We are either "at home" and in deep connection to our self, to others, to nature, to our environment and the world, and to the universe itself, in whose infinite space we exist; or we are lost and alone in a way that often leaves us confused, isolated, fearful and ashamed. It is when the pain of our own wounding is at its height, that we believe most in our own loneliness.

Though we all sing different notes of the same love song, when we are still and silent, we discover that we all share the same broken-heartedness. We face the same exile from our true relatedness to Life's love for us. Our movement back towards the truth of this

The charity of suffering

connection, for a moment here and a moment there, makes us whole again. We are returned home through the sacred charity of suffering.

* * *

A deep acceptance of my own vulnerability allows me to rest in the stillness of my own being. It is a place where the healing light of everlasting Love shines most brightly. Yet, for all my longing, it is not an easy thing to allow.

The restoration of our secret fidelity to the eternal Oneness of all life comes when we face the intimacy of our own wounding and find once more the true beauty of Being. We are shown that all aspects of our shared humanity exist together and are held as one in the loving intelligence of our compassion.

* * *

To know this connection through my own experience brings my suffering into a wider, more profound context. Beyond the claustrophobic confinement and confusion of the personal, it reveals its deeper meaning and source.

I begin to see where all my confusing, negative behaviour has its origin. Silence and my own loving presence offers me a new depth of relatedness within myself.

We see that we are not the centre of our own suffering; that this is not the whole truth. We notice we are drawn most strongly towards connection through our shared vulnerability. In the midst of this healing, we find closeness, love and kindness towards others and we learn what it is to suffer together in the holy presence and eternal flow of Charity.

Love and the Sacred Song of the Hedgerow

* * *

I cannot command the new consciousness that would allow divine Love to appear to me but my faith and humility can give me the courage to bring my own loving awareness to all in me that is wounded.

If I allow this breath of Love to pass through me, it gently brushes away the insistence upon my loneliness. The care and mercy of Silence offers me a loving witness to cradle the pain I carry.

In this tender light the blindness of my fear - and all the feelings that attach to it - are gently revealed. All that held me in darkness is swept away and a new life is reflected in the polished gold of a ceaseless fidelity to Love.

* * *

We have to become ever more deeply aware of how and when parts of who we are exclude us from the silent truth of "I am loved". The self-shame of our forsakenness appears so easily in us to create a separation that, from one moment to the next, can refuse passage to the touch of a unifying, loving Care.

To know our own suffering more consciously as the suffering of us all leads us to a faithful communion within ourselves that joins us to the humanity of all others.

* * *

In this new, inner gathering I begin to soften and break free from my defences. I am more able to reach out to others in response to their vulnerability and I can allow their compassionate movement towards

The charity of suffering

me in the midst of my own helplessness. I am more available for Love to find me. I begin to enter the flowing river of Charity that pours itself through all life.

Allowing the deepest experience of this sacred giving to penetrate us, introduces the living context of unity and Love into the process of our healing connection.

The light of each human soul shines out in the depth to which this holy generosity and forgiveness can inhabit our perception in an expansive field of loving Care that encompasses the deepest level of being human.

* * *

We see that all creation is not a unity of separate identities and classifications but the eternal dance of one movement that has its source far beyond our influence. The unspoken truth of this is to be found in the depth and unity of our own being. We have to find a way to shine our own loving light into the darkness of all we hide, in order to discover the secret buried deep in the innermost sanctuary of our own pain.

As we become more and more receptive to the mercy of this look upon us, we refuse to accept the falsehood of our separateness and isolation.

Every moment of letting go carries the influence of divine Love. All our deepest desires belong to the divine longing that is eternally pouring itself out as an invincible Charity, into all life.

From doing into being, from isolation to connectedness, from contracted and defended to open and receptive, from the head into

Love and the Sacred Song of the Hedgerow

the vast empire of the heart; it is Love that allows all these opposites to meet in the sanctity of our own embodied attention. In the silence that makes this possible, our suffering is recognised as the secret gateway to the one breath and the one heart that loves us into being.

**Love means that which lasts forever
If Love comes, it never goes.
If it goes, it is not Love.**

Maharaj Charan Singh Ji

May

The sun has broken through after three days of thick cloud. Now, instead of a ceiling of grey, the wide blue of East Anglian sky is made wider still by drifting white cumulus. It is a warm evening. Wild grasses brush my legs as I walk and, here and there, carpets of buttercups and speedwell spread patches of bright yellow and pale blue along the track. The borders of the footpaths are filled with cow parsley and pink and white campion. The leaves of the Ash, always the last to arrive, are newly soft and virgin-green.

All is praise. The hawthorn, May queen of the hedgerow and keeper of its deepest secrets, bows to Love. The soft pinkness of her blossom melts her surrender into beauty.

This sacred obedience binds us all. It beckons us deeper. It strips away all our defences and raises our vulnerability to the light until our wounding flies free from its own captivity. Nature brings us to the welcome of all that we are and the hawthorn celebrates our union in the confetti of her flowers.

This queen opens my heart to the mystery and the sanctity of the hedgerow, crowned in the charity of giving and receiving. I feel her command for homage and fealty and for my vow of loyalty to Love.

A quarrel of sparrows cease their noisy chatter as I pass and flutter away to the safety of the branches I have left behind me. In the sudden silence, I can hear in the distance the church bells of St Mary's calling the faithful home. Bird, bell, blossom and me, held in the same summons.

Chapter 6
Surrender

Love is sacrifice. We are whispered into being by the breath of Love. All that is infinite and eternal pours itself into each moment of our finite lives. In the midst of this unconditional giving, we too are called to surrender ourselves to all that offers itself to us as Love so that we can become baptised in the reciprocity of a sacred Charity.

We are revealed as Consciousness, Love and Beauty, through our mind, heart and body, in our thought, feeling and action. This living trinity of trinities guides us to the fullest expression and purpose of what it is to be human.

* * *

From the deep inward journey into our own compassionate self-knowledge and healing, our inner unity flows into life as love for our neighbours on earth and as a testament to our kinship in the infinite.

To love is the first of all commandments. The second is to be still so

Surrender

that faith can complete its bridge of light across the unknown to the knowledge of what it is to be eternally loved.

Only in the grace of this awakening are we free to sing our own sacred note in the symphony of Oneness. This turning to express, in joy and praise, the life of our individuality can only resound in the silence of Faith and the might of our surrender to Love's Will.

* * *

Yet deep stillness is hard won. I live in my own noise, my defences always pointing towards the urgency and fear of what might come. As protection, I push ahead of me all my knowing, my attitudes and opinions, my habits and actions and refuse to countenance any contradiction that would rock the foundations of what is comfortable, familiar and safe.

* * *

I try to find Love by myself without understanding that the minute I bring my will to the battle, I face my inevitable defeat. All effort on my part is to let go, to loosen the hold of the protective power of my ego and allow it to be gently penetrated by sacred forces that will guide it to its submission...

... and yet, I am forever afraid of the price to be paid. Love would strip me of everything I hold most dear - all my desires save for it alone, all that I know and everything that protects and asserts how I think my self to be.

Only the humility of my helplessness and vulnerability allows Love passage, as a light that shines through my darkness back to a peace that prevails against all pain and all joy.

Love and the Sacred Song of the Hedgerow

* * *

How do we dare to obey the truth of who we are and accept the ruthless ultimatum of eternal Love? After all, the last time we presented ourselves in our innocence, as candidates to receive the embrace of all that is boundless and unconditional, we became prey to the limitations and the uncertainty of worldly love.

The dread of that memory lies buried in every cell, thought, feeling and impulse we have ever experienced. As we go in search of others for our happiness and fullness-of-being, we carry with us our fear of being discovered.

* * *

The abyss that divides me from Love demands I let go of all my past and my clinging to safety and, instead, leap into the dark with nothing but a fragile faith that an unseen hand will reach out to catch me.

We can know Love once we believe in it: the mind can never agree to that. It demands proof in advance. Only the heart can find the courage to leap naked into the dark light of new becoming.

All that we imprison in shame confirms our unloveableness. Only the heart has the ability to surrender its safety and risk stepping towards a Forgiveness beyond our own longing.

* * *

All that we seek - all the love we could ever want - is already here, animating every moment of our becoming, yet the drama of a life lived unconsciously drags us away from the deep ground of a silent heart, in which the treasure of who we are is to be found.

Surrender

Love is an eternal stillness of Being that can never disappear; neither can it force itself upon us. It must wait until there gathers within us the still silence in which Love can be known as that which we are in our deepest essence.

In the intimacy of that surrender, we are illuminated by the Unity to which we belong.

Our faith is to offer up all our trust to that place in us where the truth "rings true". We have no other choice but to turn towards what we "feel" is there, in the loving Care of a Presence waiting beyond all time for us to accept it.

Our destiny and our journey to find that Presence lie in the depth of our selves. Once there, lifted up by a love of consciousness, we become known. Love is the surrender of everything in us to our own vastness, which can only happen in the vastness of Love surrendering itself to us.

In the immoveable stillness that lies behind all our thinking and doing, with our deep attention held fast, we are shown what Being and Love are.

The sacred mirror of life, in which we are reflected, shows us the richness of our poverty in all we don't wish to see: not just our loneliness and loss but all the ways in which we keep our vulnerability at bay and, through that defensive prowess, isolate ourselves and cause suffering to others.

To give myself away demands complete sincerity and courage.

Love and the Sacred Song of the Hedgerow

Nothing about me can be hidden or excluded. Before I leap, I have to rediscover my faith in the luminous Mercy that rises out of the dark, still moment.

* * *

I have to submit to all my thoughts and impulses and feelings being exposed and, in that most precious of moments, I see it is my own shame and guilt and fear of judgement that does not consent to Love's infinite forgiveness.

This is the door to eternity in the beauty of transformation - the "crucifixion" and resurrection awaiting us in each moment of our lives - offered by Love pressing itself upon us, demanding from us all that it gives of itself.

* * *

We can begin to offer ourselves to this Love by discovering who we already are: we become faithful to the eternal by agreeing to see ourselves through the warmth of our own loving self-awareness. The greater our humility and self-compassion, the more brightly we reflect Love in all its greatness.

This opening is the first step. It is in the Stillness that we become more and more aware of the sacred touch of a wordless Presence.

* * *

How do we let go all our self-protection and in our nakedness freely give ourselves to be baptised in the ocean of this still faith? Love bids us ascend further and further into the truth of being, which is revealed in our own lives when we agree to allow the living light of

Surrender

awareness to penetrate the secret shadows we hold beyond the reach of our welcome.

In the freedom of our humility, we submit to a Love that awakens us to ourselves. Our faith can be expressed in our desire to become more loving: to be that which we seek.

* * *

We are able to nurture the qualities of love so that the divine can recognise its home in us and can begin to deepen our way of being in our behaviour to others and towards ourselves. As we cultivate the virtues of love, we learn again to be lived by Love. This is our journey.

In stillness I begin to see all that arises in me in response to a divinity that can touch its gentle truth upon my finite life and illumine my thoughts and feelings. In this silence, the presence of Love can heal my pain, my fear and my loneliness.

* * *

Love is all I can ever trust. Whatever level of love I come to know in the everyday world of my life, the experience leaves me more open and expansive; and in these moments of grace I am brought closer to that which is beyond my knowing.

The touch "from above", if we enter into the stillness and mystery of that movement, is always loving. Whenever something of a "higher" consciousness gives itself away to something that has a denser quality than itself, it is experienced as an expansion of space or clarity or deeper insight, full of loving kindness. We know it as a mercy that always welcomes us into the Light. No one is ever refused the forgiveness. All in us that was lost to the light is honoured.

Love and the Sacred Song of the Hedgerow

* * *

Our prodigality and the long, painful journey back from the memory of our banishment are met in celebration of our homecoming. Our loneliness and loss and all that we have felt as shameful, can finally receive its loving welcome in the sacred embrace of all that gathers around our hearts.

We feel the current of a new life surrendered to the flow of the ocean. Silent and faithful, our heads bowed, we are revealed as Love by the holy gaze upon us.

Part Three

Summer

The Symphony of All Things

There is nothing that is not Love. Everything is here in its own completion. Everything is home. White galleon clouds sail across a sea of blue and swallows dance with the wind.

It is in our own summer that we can find the joy of what we can become. Our flowering and our fullness bring us to the destiny of our own note in the symphony. We are awake to the season of our wholeness. We have been painted by Love onto its own canvas. Now we can stand back and see the purpose of Love in the celebration of every colour and each whispered beauty.

In the deepest trembling of the heart, we can discover a sacred respect, a deference for all that gives itself to us. The laws of creation flow through our wish to be and we discover that we belong to the greatness of one Wish, sanctified in all we see.

In this summer of our perfection, true respect rises from the harmony of our own beauty and a sense of unity that is felt simply as Being. Our bodies bear witness to the truth: Everything is given to us.

The wordless Love we sense is divine Silence and Knowing penetrating and revealing all that we are. Once we feel the sweetness of this touch upon us, we have no choice but to submit to its price. In the deep of this holy encounter, we can no longer insist upon our separateness: we are lived by a divine Care that offers us all that it is so that we might serve it with all that we are, in the binding divinity of reverential surrender.

Beauty is life when life unveils her holy face.
But you are life and you are the veil.
Beauty is eternity gazing at itself in the mirror.
But you are eternity and you are the mirror.

Kahlil Gibran

June

In the shining of this new morning, the hedgerow abandons itself to its own fullness. Its gratitude gently flows through the light of all that is sacred. It attends to the divine.

The assembly in all the splendour of its summer presence, dedicates its beauty to all who see. It consecrates itself to us in celebration. All is given. It points me to the road I must take to know that same surrender in myself.

The beauty of what is in front of me brings me back to my senses and into the present. As I walk beside the hedgerow in the bright sunshine, I am shown in one moment of the heart, the unbearable loneliness in my life just a breath ago, when I was lost in thoughtlessness.

The dog rose, the great comforter and bringer of solace and hope, gathers the fullness of its wisdom on the softest breeze and the scent of its flowers carries me across the divide to all that heals. Under the force of its own self-sacrifice, I am salt dissolving in the sea. The song of a skylark strikes up in celebration of my return.

In the beauty of all that is beloved, we discover ourselves in each other. We are together; we are joy, living in the holiness of nature as the one inexhaustible grace of giving and receiving.

I can feel the sacrament of Love in the warmth and the light, pressing themselves against my skin.

Chapter 7
The Prayer of Beauty

Love is beauty in the silence of its own giving. Beauty is our remembrance. It beckons us beyond our forgetting. It is Love gently pressing its holiness upon us through each of our senses and calling upon our hearts to give themselves to all that is giving itself to us.

> Beauty is Love sharing the song of its own joy. The divine silence of its music calls us to enter the poetry of our own being.

* * *

> In moments of openness, the veil of all that separates us falls away and Life reveals the truth of the unity to which we belong. In the stillness of Space in which Love moves, we are revealed as nothing without Love.

> Beauty is the holy intimacy of our surrender to Love surrendering itself to us. It is the gifted harmony and joy of Love, flowing through the sacred unity of everything that is.

Love and the Sacred Song of the Hedgerow

A thought, a feeling, a mountain, a wave upon the sea, the tender expansion of a cell, the slightest beat of a heart, a wing upon the wind, the laughter in children's eyes, and the motion of the planets - all are unified by their own beauty in the holiness of Being.

All that gathers between us and connects our hearts to one another flows across the same divine eternity of Space to be met by the audience of our senses.

* * *

All that has ever been, all that is happening now and all that has yet to happen, takes its place in the communion of Oneness. We are boundless beyond our sight, smell, taste, touch, hearing and perception; beyond the material, beyond our knowing; beyond our sorrows and our joys.

This body of ours may feel separate and "mine" but it belongs to the Love that animates it in the cradle of a timeless Space through which all that exists is Love.

* * *

Everything created shares the same birth in the beauty of life and Love. We are nature. We are our source in the embodied intimacy of the still heart of the soul that does not beat to any time. We are beauty in search of itself.

We are being born in the perfection of every moment, yet we are constantly trying to create beauty by ourselves. The legacy of our lives is to allow all that is truly creative to flow through us as inspiration and harmony and as a freedom that brides itself to the eternal laws of Love.

The Prayer of Beauty

* * *

All nature gives itself without thought to the eminence of the present moment. Only we - the one creature who reaches for a consciousness beyond our own - can become lost and found again. Only we can know what it is to have our blindness lifted from us by Love. In that moment, we move from destroyers to become the heralds of a loving Care for all around us.

Every taste, sound and sight, every smell, touch and perception, when it is offered free passage through our hearts, allows the precious messenger of our body to bring word that all life is prayer.

In that moment of grace, we submit to the quiet command of creation in all that is beautiful and our bodies can receive the intimacy of the universe in which they are held and so allow us to discover our source.

* * *

Beauty is Love's call to us to awaken our hearts and free ourselves from the prison of all passing things. It holds us fast to the sacredness and living joy of all that yields.

Opening to every impression reveals the vulnerability Love demands of us. Our defences must fall and the humility of surrender take their place. Our hearts are brought alive in their awakening to the divine presence of Love in the very gathering and embrace of a simple hedgerow.

* * *

Beauty is the sacrament of the infinite in us and in all things in the revelation of giving and receiving that is Love itself.

Love and the Sacred Song of the Hedgerow

In this state of receptivity the body can finally know its own gratitude. Our beauty resonates to the beauty of nature and we unite in our shared kinship. We become the seen, the tasted, the smelled, the heard, the felt and the perceived. We submit to the enchantment nature offers us in our shared abandonment to Being.

Beauty is a radiance that seeks only itself. It leads us gently to the everlasting compassion of infinite Space through which all life flows and in which the eternality of Love and the fleeting mercy of our bodies share their joy in each other.

* * *

Something is being lived in these moments beyond the reach of our six sacred senses. It is the gift of Love being poured into us without end, calling us back to our immortality.

Now, in the fullness of our own lives, patiently attentive, the melody of a sacred music can be played through us in the wonder, joy and endless expression of our own servant individuality.

* * *

The perfection of summer grasses jewelled by rain, the trembling of a soft wind through leaves, clouds painted by a sunset, white mountains reflected in the innocence of a still lake - it is through this beauty that nature calls us to the prayer of its own enfolding.

In return, it asks only for the reverence of our senses and the blessing of our thankfulness for the grace of all abundance and generosity.

Beauty opens us to the sacrament of our senses. All that we take into the heart allows the flow of beauty to meet the beauty that flows in us. All that our senses receive becomes the sacred gift of who we are.

The Prayer of Beauty

* * *

In the final truth of beauty, Love unfurls within us and we see and feel all that is infinitely precious in nature is also infinitely precious in us.

When we become conscious of this living flame of light within us, we are free to belong again to the fountain of all Being that has its source in Love.

We feel a divine giving in the immediacy of each embodied moment. All life is penetrated by Love. Even in its ugliness and lostness, Life holds within it the beauty of its harmony and justice, waiting to be seen in the gratitude of all nature for its own being. These moments are prayer. Nothing is separate from Love. Everything is held in the compassion of an eternal Care, especially all that is lost.

* * *

All life is a sacred movement towards relationship. Fear forces us into exile but even fear has access to the beauty of what is to be found deep within its own trepidation.

It is in our separation from Love that we discover the strength of our longing. The grace of all that offers itself as our healing is graced, in return, by the humility of our troubled heart.

* * *

Beauty builds its own shining bridge of light across the abyss and calls us home to our loving wholeness. Life reveals itself as Love and Love waits for the secret depths of our hearts to awaken to its eternal summons.

Love and the Sacred Song of the Hedgerow

In each moment of being found, Love flows through us and sweeps away all our desires but one. In the boundless Space of all creation, we become the beauty and perfection of all that loves us.

Through the divinity of abundance and the generosity of all that sustains us, we become the earth and the earth dissolves into the immensity of our own hearts.

* * *

In these moments of meeting, the presence of the Divine surrenders itself to us and, without waiting for our consent, draws the living gratitude of our own heart to the beauty offering itself to us.

Just as each petal knows the presence of the ocean in the gentle touch of a raindrop, so we, too, are being whispered home by beauty through each of our senses in the living temple of our own bodies.

All that we do carries us towards this sacred unity, yet all that we are has its source beyond the reach of our senses. Here, beauty becomes faith, and, in the stillness that reveals a divine Care for us, we come to know the infinite through the holy resonance of our own being.

* * *

The sacred Charity that animates our body, mind and feeling is the Love that animates all life. Beauty illuminates the gift of all that is given - including all with which we struggle. In this intimacy, held in the heart, Oneness is revealed to us as the grace and eminence of every breath.

In the divine Space of this present moment Love takes us to itself in patience, loving kindness, forgiveness and mercy, and we become the adornment of its own praise.

**I, the fiery life of divine essence, am aflame
beyond the beauty of the meadows. I gleam in the
waters.
I burn in the sun, moon, and stars.
With every breeze, as with invisible life that contains
everything,
I encourage blossoms to flourish with ripening fruits.
I am the rain coming from the dew that causes the
grasses to laugh**

Hildegard of Bingen

July

There is a cloudless blue sky this morning. A warm breeze plays its mischief through the leaves of the Wayfarer tree.

This is a tree of homecoming, whose mystical rowan heart breaks us free from the lost ways of old thinking to honour our true potential. It lifts the spirits of those of us who are lost to our hearts and sees us safely home to Love's path.

If we place ourselves in its care and rest in the patience of its command, it tells us to be still, to find the way. I pay attention to what I am being taught by the cream flowers of its Spring and by the bright blood of its summer berries that will soon turn autumn-black. Birth and death are alive in the silence of eternity and the Wayfarer will not hide the truth of its lesson from all wayward travellers who pass-by.

It points me back towards the home of my wandering heart and offers me the courage to face a reckoning whose coming is already hinted by the ripening of the corn.

This sentinel tree walks beside me when I lose my way and guides my footsteps back to my place in the certainty and beauty of birth and death that lives in the heart of the hedgerow's silent teaching.

A little Blackcap struck up the sweetest love song. My heart and his mate, far enough away for me not to see her, both answered.

Now, the Wayfarer, minstrel of all the other trees, sings the stillness of its own truth to the bird and to me:
    "Listen! I am the secret of your way home".

Chapter 8
The loving touch of Attention

Love is our Praise. Every one of us is our own living search for Love. The knowledge sealed in all our longing, when taken into the heart, becomes the wisdom of Love. It is the secret that holds us in its divine poise between the answer we seek and the question that brings it alive.

Love waits for us to turn the soft touch of our attention towards its presence and know ourselves in the prayer of all that is everlasting.

* * *

The boundless joy of infinite Love reverberates across space and time when we bring the healing welcome of our loving attention to all in us that has felt loveless.

All those precious parts of us that still live in exile from the sacred flow of creation are the cause of all divine suffering. Our grief for all we have ever lost holds within it our sacred homesickness.

The loving touch of Attention

Every wound we bear can find its rest in the depth of an unknowable, sanctifying Attention that brings with it the cathedral of one simple truth: you are loved; you have always been loved; and you will always be loved.

* * *

The voice of our loyalty to Love sounds again in our hearts when we offer the gentleness of our care and attention to the suffering we carry in us.

We move from the contraction of our fear and reactivity to the inner space and compassion of a new resonance. We become our own loving companion, opening us to a unity of oneness that has always been here, hidden within us in every desire we have ever had.

* * *

The grace of our own unconditional, loving regard brings us ever closer to the homecoming our wounding longs for, as we submit to the poetry of our forgiveness, which echoes an infinite Forgiving.

Love enters our consciousness in the silence of a heart that is open, receptive and vulnerable. So often, though, we are confronted by the castle walls of our fear.

When our hearts retreat to the dread of not being loved, the divine current of becoming, to which we belong, recedes further and further from our awareness.

We are haunted by the memory of our banishment. Our self-protection from this pain separates us from the infinite embrace and Mercy of all that is true.

Love and the Sacred Song of the Hedgerow

* * *

To belong again to the joy of a boundless Love, I must let go the defences that lock me in the prison of my own wounding.

Through the journey of our lives, we are destined to carry with us the tyranny of a loyal ego that will always insist upon its separateness. All that is wounded and fearful has to be welcomed back to its true home.

The sacred music of compassion sounds through the infinite space of everything existing when we offer ourselves the warmth and understanding of our own loving attention. In that moment a new receptivity allows us to feel another Attention act upon us. This Attention is always pouring out its love as divine Sorrow for our suffering.

* * *

The liberation of offering up the weight of our burden to the loving care of this Attention brings its holy light to the trinity of our presence.

Its deep gaze upon us reveals three distinct inner gravities-of-being that govern our lives with their three separate states of consciousness. Our deepest healing is to be found in their unity. Our lostness to Love lies in the splintered trinity of their fragmentation. Only our dedication to discovering what Love is can awaken the forces that guide us back to our holiness.

The first of the three, the one with the strongest pull, lives in the pain and illusion of not being loved. Our first primal, infant rupture from the unconditional oneness of Love happens through a wide variety of

The loving touch of Attention

unintentional woundings and sometimes from the shattering of intentional ones.

* * *

There is no escape from suffering. The gossamer sensitivity of our virgin innocence registers even the slightest pulling away of love's gaze. We are haunted by a gathering shame when we are 'corrected' by a loving, parental care that seeks to prepare us for a life of right and wrong.

The power of moments like these - almost imperceptible to adults - imprison us in the dread of our own foresakenness. The secret of our unworthiness and our fear of it being seen govern the actions of this first, infant centre of our being, as we strive, from behind our hiding, for for the best of us to be seen and loved.

* * *

Until this hostage child in us is joined by the resources and spiritual understanding of the other two centres, we are forever lost to the healing knowledge that we are not our wounding; and that our suffering beckons us beyond the drama of each day to the timeless reality of our lives and to the wisdom of the divine Sorrow we carry in our hearts.

If we are pulled into the exile of this first centre and lived by the history of our young hurt, then our journey through life is filled with all our confusion, doubt, blindness and reactivity that push through into our lives as hidden fear and anger. In this state, we are spring tides lost to their moon.

* * *

Love and the Sacred Song of the Hedgerow

The second gravity-of-being offers us access to a broader, more empowered awareness. We could call it the present awareness of our adult being. It is the archivist of the whole story of our lives and relationships and it can harness the reassurance of the truth - that we have, in fact, survived all that has been visited upon us. We are still here; still held by the sacred loyalty of our search for Love.

In the presence of this more expansive and empowered way of seeing myself, I can witness all that arises from my young vulnerability. In these moments, the possibility of choosing not to go with the reactive pull of my past offers me the miracle of a new freedom.

* * *

My infant place of fear will always be triggered into the present by the threat of judgement and rejection but now I have the choice not to be drowned in the flood of its pain. It no longer governs my behaviour.

When I bring the loving gentleness of my attention to all that is happening in me, I discover that I am not only my body, my feelings, or my thoughts. Instead, I can hold each of them in the wisdom and freedom of this new inner gaze.

We now gain access (often with the help of another) to a new way of seeing ourselves: we find a greater clarity-of-understanding in our witnessing of the way in which we have met life from feelings of the past that are no longer true in this present moment.

* * *

The touch of our own loving attention grants us access to a depth of compassion that is always awake in the third of our three gravities of being - the true heart of all in us that belongs to eternal Love. From

The loving touch of Attention

here, the deepest sanctuary of our knowing, the gentle embrace of a new acceptance offers its gift to all that we judge in ourselves. We begin to love what we meet from the sacred influence of our true Self.

The wordless knowledge of our divine belonging to the infinity of Love rests in this centre of our being. From here, Love can come alive in the witness of a sacred Attention.

In the grace of this new seeing, we are made ready. We are able to care for ourselves in the wisdom of loving kindness. We prepare the way for the divinity of a new wholeness by reclaiming these exiled parts of us and transforming their pain and suffering through the light of our own care and regard.

The long wait is over. We feel the soft touch of the love and welcome we have longed for our whole lives.

In this moment of our resurrection, each centre of being reaches out to the other and in their holy communion we sense the presence of a unifying Attention that has never stopped holding us in its gaze. It knows all that we are and bathes us in the loving Care of its divine Heart.

Once we enter this new flow of life in the present moment, we give up trying to imagine our lives into the shapes we want them to be and, instead, we invite the world around us to reveal itself just as it is.

Now, we can live in the humility of Being. We are part of this wholeness, not different or separate but alive in the Oneness of our being to all Being.

Love and the Sacred Song of the Hedgerow

In this holiness, instead of looking for Love, we are Love. Instead of being mortal, we know our immortality in the kindred spirit of all creation.

The aliveness of this praise finds its highest expression, through us, as the deep humility of our loving attention, anchored in a sacred peace behind all that we do.

* * *

This silence includes everything. There is no 'sacred this" and "profane that". Nothing is loveless. Rather, it is lost to Love or lost to our attention. To seek this wholeness is a grace given by infinite Love as its own longing.

Wherever life or my thoughts take me, however much I become distracted and identified, it is infinitely surpassed by all that is given to me here, in this present moment, that testifies to the reality of Love.

Under the look of my own loving attention, all my wounding is included. Love forever wraps itself around all suffering - not to take it away but to light our way through the infinite touch of Mercy and Compassion.

* * *

Where once we lived our lives in the secret shame of loss, now in the grace of Attention we become loyal to what is eternal in the never-ending truth of a Love always alive in us.

All that is form now exists to express the sacred wholeness of Love. Through the loving touch of this new way of seeing, we become

The loving touch of Attention

Love's praise. Nature is the honoured herald of this truth, as the bringer of all its power and beauty to our world.

From the trinity of our inner unity, Love opens us completely to the truth of suffering in the world and guides us to the grace of loving kindness, forgiveness and the still presence of a faith that surrenders us to Love's Will.

* * *

Once here, we have no choice but to offer up our comfort and help from hearts that are opened wide to the suffering of others. The beauty of all these acts of the heart connects us to a divine Care that will forever bring us its comfort and help: suddenly, the resonance of a truth beyond our knowing becomes our own.

We are that which we seek and which seeks us. We see that, wherever our attention is led, it carries with it the chalice of a longing for love that is the deepest echo of Love's longing for us.

**I come to my love
As dew on the flowers**

Mechtild of Magdeburg.

August

The sun is shining but there has been so much rain over the last two weeks that a lot of the wheat fields still haven't been harvested.

All along the hedgerow, in the warmth and the wet, the field maple and hazel, the blackthorn and field elm are pushing out beyond their own boundary. Young branches, in love with life, spread themselves wide into the welcome of space and the late summer air.

The crab apple, ancient bringer of wisdom and surprise, has the union of the four seasons buried in its pink wood. It recites marriage vows in front of the congregation of all that is ripening.

Close by, the dogwood stands patiently watching its berries paint themselves to red. Wild plums are turning browny-green but, like the blackberries, are not yet sweet enough to eat.

House martins sweep low over the damp wheat as it crackles in the hot sunshine. They are gathering for their long flight home to Africa.

Time is slowly sewing its stitches through the folds of the hedgerow's cloth. The silent wisdom of the crab apple speaks the secret of our inseparability from the timeless movement of Love in all nature. In the everlasting Care of each moment it tells me: "Be present to this eternity. You will not pass this way again!".

Chapter 9
Goodness

Love is the mercy of each moment. The banquet of Love's melody fills our lives with joy when we accept the grace of divine Care as our sacred, everlasting help. Each movement towards the soft light of this loving Goodness embodies its own profoundly significant moment of mercy.

To live on the gentle breath of a gracious life is the unfolding of a sacred practice, like the bud of a new rose that holds the beauty and perfection of all flowers yet to bloom.

* * *

In all that we do, in all its wonderful creative vitality and variety, the reality of our oneness expresses itself in all that is peaceful, patient and kind. Here, we enter the realm of the heart in all the holiness of its simplicity.

To feel the mercy of Goodness in our lives (in our thoughts and the feelings of our heart and in the movements of our body) transforms all

Goodness

our striving and straining into the joyfulness of love, wisdom, kindness, beauty and the ecstasy of abundance.

I can learn to bring the sanctity of my own care and attention to all that I do in my life, as an act of faith and fidelity to the divine Care that is permeating all of us every moment of our becoming.

* * *

The sacred obedience of the hedgerow gifts me a Light through which I can discover the humility of my gratitude to all that is nature and to the living world of plenty that is our home planet.

* * *

Goodness and Care stretch far beyond our own lives. We can accept their mercy for ourselves but they are not ours to possess. Love wishes to flow through us and not to be held hostage: divine Care dances in the freedom of its joy.

When we do not imprison this holy Goodness as 'mine', it becomes our harmony, our healing and our service. We become Good.

To accept the blessing of each gracious moment turns us towards the divinity of wholeness and allows us to engage more fully in the communion of life from all within ourselves that recognises the Divine.

* * *

This source of uniting every aspect of our lives to all that is pure and eternal can be felt in the heart as "help from above". It can come to us as a new attentiveness to what we are and do, and it can appear as the grace of being loved by Life itself...and,

Love and the Sacred Song of the Hedgerow

more profoundly, in the blessing of serving that Love and that Life.

The sacred offering we receive blends its Goodness into the simplicity and holiness of placing our hands together, making tea, getting dressed in the morning, and in all the ways we place ourselves in relationship to the world around us.

Loving Care is a gateway between our two worlds. Each ritual of our day can become a welcome for the presence of the eternal to take its place in our lives and, in that moment, we join the giving and receiving of life's sacred prayer. Love delights in its own discovery in all we do.

* * *

Paying attention to the Care that is paying attention to us, brings into our lives a new and radical sense of peace.

I can begin to offer the care of my own loving attention to my body, my health, my home, my environment and to all the vulnerability of my feelings - not to have them bound in the rigid discipline of ought's and should's, but as a natural, flowing goodness in my life.

When we accept the loving help of divine Care, the soft rose of compassion and self-compassion begins to flower within us without any sentimentality or any investment in an outcome. We become loyal to serving the flow of Goodness in the world by, first, allowing it to flow in us.

* * *

The limitless outpouring of Love, giving itself to us in the grace of

Goodness

each breath, frees us to enter into a celebration of relationship to ourselves, each other, to life and to the planet, which hosts us.

Once it enters the prism of everyday life, the gentle response of our loving attention refracts its rainbow colours into all our relationships with our friends, family, work, and nature and into all life around us. The light of this joyful goodness also spreads through the intimacy of our body, thoughts and emotions.

The quiet watchfulness of our own attentive care brings with it a quality of awareness and meekness that establishes in us a sense of balance, a stillness of purpose ,and the kindness of simplicity.

Goodness shines through the inner movements of softening, opening and widening. We discover peace in the letting go of tensions and strivings. It is a movement inwards of a certain kind of gentleness that expands our awareness of what is present in the sanctity of this moment. Usually, we are too distracted by thoughts, emotions, sensations or external attractions, to feel what is true.

Through the grace of our surrender, we move from a world of separate things to one of unity. We soften into the deep heart of caring and loving relationship. We learn to take joy in the sacred Goodness of this infinite Care for us that serves all life.

I can see and feel when something harsh enters into my reaction to the external and internal happenings that reach my awareness…and, in that holy, yet fleeting moment of all that is graced, I am able to allow another influence to act upon me.

Love and the Sacred Song of the Hedgerow

I can breathe gently into my body. I can slow down and become quieter. As I move towards stillness, I see what in me is not still and I can bring the gratitude of my own loving awareness as a response to being granted the grace to see that.

* * *

Hallowing the joy of Goodness in a way that allows the infinite to enter and draw us into its Care can only happen when we allow all that we do to be held in the silence of the witnessing heart.

The quiet gathering of my attention and care opens me to the deep humility of Life and to a sense of harmony and inner order from which can come a radiance of action in the sacred force of every gesture.

By devoting ourselves to a gracious life we become something greater than just ourselves. Through the temple of our bodies, all that touches the heart of our awareness becomes our path and our praise.

* * *

Moving towards the world with the intention to be gentle and kind, breaks the fortress walls of all our defences. When we try to become gentler, more understanding and more merciful towards our self (especially to those aspects of us that we have been taught to enshame), we are released from the persecution of judging ourselves and others and brought towards a new tenderness of heart.

This gentleness becomes, of itself, a deeply powerful practice that allows us to link here, in this very moment – however briefly or distantly - to the freedom of all that is more loving.

* * *

Goodness

To become gentle and kind in the way we talk, act and treat our self, and others, brings with it a joy of a life joined to a greater, more essential world of fellowship and unity. We become more permeable to the enervating, revitalising and renewing power of all the Care that waits to celebrate with us our entry into a divine Life.

* * *

Right now, here in this moment, what is it that I love? If I let the radicality of this question become the daily foundation of my practice, it will bring me face-to-face with the power and the strength of everything that distracts me from the holiness of my life.

My attention loves whatever it is drawn to. How, then, do I allow it to be drawn to the Goodness of all that is sacred?

The invitation to experience the Divine is there in everything we see. The gift of the sacred is to be discovered in every action and every movement of life, when Grace grants us our freedom to see. It awakens in us the vitality of faith and animates the eternal presence of all that is Good.

* * *

In particular, we can be brought alive to a compassion for all those we see who are still fearful of opening to the fullness and abundance of life: we witness, through them, how the darkness of fear and separateness obscures and obstructs all our attempts to move towards a sense of deeper connection. We become the pupil and they our teachers of what it is to be human.

* * *

To be gentle in all we do demands courage. It inevitably links us to

Love and the Sacred Song of the Hedgerow

our vulnerability but the acknowledgement of our own limitation opens us to an inexhaustible source of help, there in the holiness of all we know to be Good.

We begin to accept life as it is without the confinement of our wanting and wishing for things to go the way of our own will.

The more loving Care appears in our lives, the more beautiful we become. Our caring begins to turn us towards our source and origin. We begin to learn the power of meekness and the new world we create shines its light through the darkness of all in us that is fearful and still living in the illusion of being alone.

* * *

Our care opens the door to the loving flow of Goodness in life. Through its action we can allow love, kindness and compassionate attentiveness to express themselves, joyfully, in all we are and do.

Divine Care is forever pouring itself out into our lives but its gift will never belong to us. As the precious emissaries of this Care for us, we can know its Goodness only by giving it away. From the humility and gratitude of an open heart, we offer our own care where we see it is most needed. In the gentle grace of that seeing and the Mercy of that moment, we are made Good.

Part Four

Autumn

The Harvesting

We are the harvesters and the harvest. The deep abundance of the hedgerow is freely offered as its sacrifice to all hearts that would open. The timeless compassion of its giving shines its light into the coming darkness.

The discipleship of these autumned trees preaches its gospel to those who pass. They would have me know that the fulfilment of all that is holy lies not just in the beauty of their growth and generosity but in the covenant of their mortality, the true revealer of life in all its precious completeness.

The still silence of death laughs at all our attempts to govern life. Its dark wisdom gently whispers us free from the lives we would lead according to our own will and turns us to the sincerity of devotion, reverence and prayer - the harvest of our own lives, offered back through the death of our self-separateness.

The truth of all that passes away protects us from believing in the success of living life on our terms. We cannot defy it. We cannot escape the pain of not lasting, yet the secret embrace of our acceptance opens the door to an unimaginable destiny. The reality of our transience wipes away our blindness to reveal an eternal life, governed by a divine Will.

In the continent of our own hearts, anguish, pain and sorrow are transformed into the shining secret of our salvation. Divine Sorrow watches over us in the ocean currents of a sacred Care until we see the secret of our suffering for ourselves. Death has us kneel before Love and become the harvester of our own surrender in the power of a new prayer - "thy will be done!".

As leaves fall, something in me stills.

**When you step outside and engage with the world in quiet listening, prayer will happen,
and it will take on its own way of being for you...
When I burn sage or lay tobacco down,
I know that I am tethered to a love that has remained steady throughout the centuries
and that always calls me back to its own sacredness.
And that sacredness will always lead me back out to the world to do the work of love.**

Kaitlin B. Curtice

September

There is change in the air. White clouds are high and wispy in the blue. The cold morning of the previous day gently reminds me the time of summer days is passing.

A shiver rustles the bright garments of late summer. The hedgerow knows it stands on the brink of its own withering.

The mandala of this bright September afternoon, so full of weather and hidden mysteries, wraps itself around me. Nothing is missing, nothing lost as the wind sweeps round to the south east but still presses its Saharan warmth against the flanks of the hedgerow.

The bramble, the barbed healer, brings its flame into the autumn months when the feast of its black sweetness is over. It lives by its own rules. It goes where it wants. Its tendrils embroider all the colours of fire into the living canvas of the hedgerow, weaving, uninvited but still welcomed, through the grey branches of its neighbours.

The bramble gifts the thorns of its protection to all who accept its embrace and cloaks them in its loyalty to the wind, rain, sun and snow, light and dark, warmth and cold. It cherishes all that flows in the harmony of a wholeness in which nothing is feared.

A new, darker season is returning from last year with its familiar pallet of hues and smells. The life of the hedgerow is passing through the eternity of its own fleetingness. In its silent dignity something in me relinquishes its own claim.

Chapter 10
Gladness

Love is our rejoicing. Love flows for all eternity in the golden ecstasy of its own giving. It pours itself out to us as the generosity of each moment.

We are the abundance of Love. That which is loving carries the music of a sacred Joy for all to see. The holiness of this song can only be sung by hearts that are ringing in the thankfulness and praise of Love.

Gladness is the heart giving itself away. The lantern of a divine Light shines more brightly and reveals us as our true nature in surrender and supplication. We are shown the grace of our own longing.

* * *

Thankfulness is our freedom. Everything is given. Nothing is "mine". When we are the harvest of Love, everything becomes a sacred exchange. We breathe in Love's tender Care for us and we breathe out our homage and our trust in the gift of the next breath.

Love and the Sacred Song of the Hedgerow

Every time we turn towards Love, we discover Love is already turned towards us.

We can touch an essential longing in us to give ourselves to that Love, giving itself to us. By becoming more thankful for all that we see, we draw ever closer to the fire of Love in which we are no longer distinct but are rejoiced by the one Longing in the ocean of Light that unites all Life.

* * *

Through the Grace of gratitude, I discover an intimation of something in me that must be offered up to divine Mercy. To allow Love to express itself through the living of my own life, I first abandon everything I wish to acquire for myself. Gladness is the freedom in which I willingly give myself away to the summons of a greater Will. I let go of all my independence in an act of reverence and deep appreciation for the granting of each new day.

Divine Joy shines out into our lives as the vastness to which we belong. Once it flames in us, it brings the peace and the stillness of homecoming. In that moment, there is only one abundance living itself through us, in, and as, the giving and receiving of Love.

* * *

However much we struggle to give ourselves away to Love, it is Love's surrender to us that restores the innocence of our own yielding. This tribute of the self is paid, little by little. Every time we leave the safe shore of our conclusions and turn towards the wild ocean of our heart, we are moved closer to the embrace of infinite Love. Every time we are pulled away by distraction, we become lost again in the illusion of all that is separate.

Gladness

In the mystery of an unknown Mercy we are loved beyond far and near, beyond good and bad, right and wrong, beyond pain and joy and all duality.

The unity of Being is giving itself to us as our very life. Once we acknowledge this sacred gift in the depth of our own gladness, the sincerity of our devotion becomes our testament.

* * *

There are still high mountains and deep valleys to cross. The ceaseless unknown of the next moment will always create a fearfulness in our minds: we build landscapes of our own likes and dislikes to guide us on our way, yet we are given the grace to surrender ourselves to a path beyond our own map.

We long ago learnt to retreat from pain and suffering but now, when we hold all that we experience - both pleasurable and painful - in our consent, we come to a new sense of meaning in the still presence of our Being.

Gladness allows us the deep acceptance of all that we are offered. When pain appears, we stay; when joy appears, we stay. When all that is given to us is held in the blessing of our gratitude, we remain anchored to an invincible quiet, as we embrace the teachings of all that comes and goes in our lives.

* * *

In the joy of Thankfulness, we are unified by the charity of receiving. All that is given sweeps away our need to possess and we feel the universal flow of our own abundance in the crystal currents of healing and creation.

Love and the Sacred Song of the Hedgerow

Embracing a life of gladness allows Love to live our lives through the infinite generosity of all that is offered us, as a loving Presence pours out the beauty of its sacrament across all eternity.

* * *

The simplicity of gladness has an immediate effect upon our lives. It is there within our reach in this present moment, just as we are and it, quite literally, brings us alive in the humility of a deep trust in the mercy and grace of Love. We cannot take it for ourselves but we live its joy.

* * *

Gratitude defies the power of my own will. I accept in the mercy of stillness the impression of every impulse that arises in me. For a very brief moment, in the grace of that seeing, I am liberated from the inevitability of reactions that push forward, heedlessly, in the blindness of their fear.

It is possible for me to hold back, just for a second, from acting automatically in whatever I do and see, think and feel, and, instead, allow myself to be touched by the grace of a new freedom. For a moment I am brought to my surrender by the merciful charity of Love. I am no longer alone.

In this liberation from the constant drama of restless fear and anxiety, we have access to the vastness of an eternal Mercy. We can experience a moment of life from a truer place in ourselves and we bring to the world action bathed in the living remembrance of Love.

* * *

In our gladness, we are free to become creative – to live more

Gladness

expansively within ourselves and to have more choice in how we act. We come closer to serving the grace and mercy of a greater Will.

In our deepest appreciation, we no longer force ahead of us the empire of our own opinions to colonise the world we see. Through the mirror of our daily life we begin to notice how we get caught in the grip of our desires and tensions and become lost again to the grace of Love's giving.

Instead, in the mystery of a sacred Silence, we gently consent to receive the impressions of the life around us and the active quality of Gladness flows into all aspects of our lives. It is a vital, powerful force in its own right, able to transform the way we live into the sanctity of what loves us.

* * *

Grace is Love received and when we know its touch upon us, in the joy of our thankfulness we become gentle and full of loving care towards ourselves and all that we see.

We are able to come into relationship with the rest of the world in a way that honours the holiness of all things. We enter the sanctuary of Being-in-Love from the fathomless deep of our own hearts.

* * *

Everything held in Love carries the gladness of its own giving. In this one great current of the Heart, death is honoured by the praise of each rebirth.

It is in the deep glory of our humility that we are harvested and become the harvest. We are alive in "you are loved", no longer insisting on our own terms; no longer here for "me". We are

Love and the Sacred Song of the Hedgerow

baptised in the sacred joy of giving that expresses its rapture in all that loves.

Our gladness is the gift of our humility. We become part of the endless, infinite flow of a sacred reciprocity that allows life to appear. Every breath is Love giving itself to us and receiving in return the glory and homecoming of each human heart.

* * *

Nothing is separate. The harvest that comes from being harvested by Love is to see our longing freed from the suffocation of separateness. Everything existing that manifests the finiteness of form is penetrated by the formless, wordless, infinite Joy of divine Love. On this new day, we welcome all that life brings. We hold all enchantment and all that is terrible to us in the secret wisdom of its deeper meaning, cradled in our gladness and trust.

We leave the safety of the shore and yield to the sanctity of the unknowable; we break free from the endless crafting of our own lives and rest in our praise of Being.

We are the harvest and the harvester of divine Sorrow and eternal Joy. We are chosen for a life no longer of our own choosing. We have been harvested by Love and have become Love.

**You are not a drop in the ocean.
You are the entire ocean
in one drop.**

Rumi

October

As I walked, the beacon of an October dawn suddenly broke through the mist and set the hedgerow ablaze in the gold of lost summer days. The delicate foliage of the field maple brings its oranges and yellows in the splendour of its turning.

In the beauty of this autumn, amidst the brightness of its many colours, new and deeper shadows begin to fall.

Sycamore seeds helicopter through the air while chestnuts and acorns - each one the womb of their own giant destiny - submit to their burial and a new birth in Spring. For now, they slumber beneath a royal blanket, woven by the gilded browns of dead autumn leaves. One day soon it will wake them from their slumber and nourish them into new life.

The chill of Winter in the first frosts has already begun its rebellion against the throne of warm days. Memory softens into the sacred poise of time and sighs its own sigh: an ending and a beginning held in the harmony and balance of a year.

The maple's deep song of enduring life, vibrates through the strings of its own harp, and a new sound gathers strength as the hedgerow exhales ever more deeply into autumn.

As I listen and look, the hand of all in me that grips too tightly begins to loosen.

Chapter 11
The justice of Humility

Love is justice. Love sings its song through each one of us, according to our own note. The more we open to the grace of humility, the more Love's melody plays through us.

The justice of humility spreads its proclamation into our lives when what we receive is determined by all that we are willing to let go. Humility is to see our true reflection in the face of Love and know what is asked of us in our nothingness without it.

* * *

The eternal gifts of Love await us when we cease to be what we desire and our hearts open to Love's will. That sacrament takes place in us when we accept the gift of all that is apportioned to us.

It is then that Love's light dispels all our darkness and shatters the illusion of our loneliness. Its peace stills our soul; its mercy forgives us all that weighs upon our heart; its grace responds to our longing for

The justice of Humility

love; its blessing accepts us as we are; its cherishing heals and calls us home.

* * *

We discover what we are when we let go the anchor of all we know. Our ego - the great guardian of all in us that remains faithful to the safe passage of our own will - imprisons us in the force of its control and protection.

Our loyal personalities are the woven armour of our past that - in straining always to keep us free from hurt - shape the structure of our lives and define the countenance we adopt in the world.

* * *

We each wish to be touched by the warmth of Love but always on our own terms. All that is personal - the canvas upon which our past is painted - carries forever the unintentional wounding at the hands of all those who influenced our early lives.

When we look more closely, we see that they, themselves, were children of children who had been led away from any understanding of the limitless Care and Oneness of Love that flows through, and transcends, all life. The secret presence of their wounds became our inheritance.

The more we are led away from the supremacy of our ego and submit to faith in the living presence of the Divine, the closer we come to the reality of what we are. Our humility heralds our opening to Love, as it draws us to itself in the sacred flow of an ancestral healing.

* * *

Love and the Sacred Song of the Hedgerow

Humility lies not just in offering up our sorrow and broken dreams to the infinite Care of Love but, also, in accepting the grace to become joyfully ourselves in the fullness of our own being, in the service of Love.

Love penetrates us all, just as we are. Everything created from the next breath or thought, to all we see, carries in it the incarnate self-giving of Love. The divine Humility of this boundless sacrifice calls our hearts to discover themselves in that same generosity.

Humility does not lie in the fear of pain or harm: it lies in the courage to face the danger of being loved and to sound the voice and meaning of that love to ourselves and to each other and to all life around us. The power of meekness - to be invincibly poor of spirit - appears in us when we accept the Grace of everything given.

* * *

When I come home to myself and bear the look of loving Attention upon me, I see that everything in me that is not alive to the spontaneity and joy of the present moment flows, instead, from the walled prison of my past.

I see that my life is governed by a reality that does not now exist, yet I unconsciously push the fearfulness of what I once knew into the innocence and welcome of what is here, now.

To sacrifice my fear is to dare to look beyond my own intent and to submit to being loved by the immensity to which we all belong - the always and endlessly loving source of divine Care submitting itself to us.

The justice of Humility

When we turn from this Love in order to dictate the outcome of our own lives, a divine Sorrow for our lostness reverberates across the Cosmos. All that is Love waits, in the infinity of eternal Patience, for us to break free from the fear that governs us, so that its Joy can be felt in the world, through us.

All in us that belongs to the source of this divine Humility weeps from the same Sorrow for our captivity. We stand there together - all that we wish for, on one side, and all we are afraid to believe in, on the other. Held down by the weight of words and concepts, our minds plead in anguish for proof of divine Love.

The mind is chained to its own ambition: once it has conclusive evidence that we are Loved from above and that it has a god on its side, then it will have access to all that power! Without this prize, we dare not believe in the Humility of the Great Desire that exists, hidden, in all that we do. We dare not trust in our hearts, even though they, alone, grant us access to the vastness of all that is eternal; and they, alone, catch the secret whisper of Love beyond all the noise and activity of our lives.

In the midst of this drama, our way of being in the world secretly plots all the comings and goings of human love in our lives until we begin to register what draws us closer to, and what takes us further away from, a conscious Love that is forever present in our lives.

From here, the sacred forgiveness of Humility pours its Care into all our brokenness and limitation, and we discover an identity that is not defined by our fearfulness. The wisdom of a new consciousness reveals the truth of who we are in Love and as Love.

Love and the Sacred Song of the Hedgerow

* * *

Can we find our way home into this new world where all our hurt and pain is held forever in a compassionate Grace, overflowing into life as the joy of our goodness?

Love thirsts for us as we thirst for it. Love stands at the door of our hearts begging to be granted admission. It waits for the first hint of our supplication to give itself completely to us, as its Mercy flowing into our lives.

* * *

Until we enter the healing current of life, we remain tied to the painful masquerade of our separateness. Our self-shame is the secret cloak of our invisibility that hides us from our own self-belief and sabotages our attempts to live in our fullness of being. In this place of shadows, we are caught in the perjury of our unworthiness.

Oh! That I would have the courage to let Love flow through me… yet only my meekness allows Love to accomplish its work, as the governing force and meaning of my life.

* * *

We are humbled by falling in love but true Love visits us from beyond the boundary of our own will. It graces us with a new consciousness that allows the Great Opening to take place in the humility and mercy of all that is still.

In the holy state of poor-in-spirit, we are granted the richness of patience, abstinence, a quiet determination, acceptance and loving kindness. Humility places us where no doing needs to be done and all is accomplished. In the beauty of this moment, we rest in the

The justice of Humility

eternal wisdom of Silence. Nothing else needs to be known and all is known.

* * *

Opening to the pain of others and sharing in their joy are the two blessings of loving kindness, carried as the resonance of our hearts to the call of Love. In the moment of this meeting, Love always answers. Its holy Forgiveness sweeps away all our fears.

When all that despairs is met by our own self-love and mercy, the Love that seeks us commands the renunciation of our unloveableness. In this moment, we become holy. In this sacred humility, we know others as ourselves and their suffering as our own. We are offered our homecoming in the sacred truth of the unity to which we belong.

* * *

Humility is the secret door to all that we are. We gain entry by passing through the unbearableness of accepting that we are destined never to find any enduring happiness in the finite world of created form. When we face the humility of that suffering, it becomes the gateway to the infinite joy of Love. Accepting the fleetingness of our lives tears down all our agendas and strategies. For a moment, we are lost to a sense of who we are until Love whispers to us to bring the care of its own loving Kindness to ourselves and to the world around us.

* * *

The power of compassion - the serene emissary of a sacred silence - reverberates down through the uniqueness of our own personal and ancestral journey into the holiest place of the heart, where the distinction of who I am no longer applies in the usual way.

Love and the Sacred Song of the Hedgerow

* * *

A new knowledge flows through us. A Love that is carried in the heart of all creation surrounds us in its joy and welcome. In our incarnated fidelity to Love's mercy, we become the key that opens the door to a Love that is limitless and everlasting.

All in us that is born to Love is awakened in the holy justice of receiving the divine Grace of all that we have given.

To be loved means to be consumed.
To love is to give light with inexhaustible oil.
To be loved is to pass away, to love is to endure.

Rainer Maria Rilke

November

The second big storm this month moved down from the north west. Rain, wind and sleet ripped the leaves from most of the trees except the oaks and beeches and the two ashes on the lee side of the hedgerow. The cold rain turned the bark of the blackthorn and field maple to black.

Most of the hedgerow has already yielded the last of its autumn colour but the tattered remnants of the ash refuse to let go their hold until the next frost. They still march to the sorcery and the drum of norse gods: Yggdrasil, the tree of life, connecting all worlds of light and shadow; the blender of opposites in the truth of its straight grain and flexibility.

The ash guides the trees around it with its torch of ageless understanding. It whispers to its neighbours as they sleep: "There is darkness now but you will wake to the light".

It is only now, as I approach the latter stages of my life, that I begin to submit to the touch of divine Love. Only now do I understand my surrender to the wisdom of my heart and the measureless ocean of Mercy and Love to which it belongs. All that it sees, all to which it gives itself, is made sacred.

As I stand on the edge of all that is unknown, it is in my heart that I can feel, running unseen through the story of my life, the gentle presence of a divine Sorrow that has forever watched over me.

It is the sacred source of my longing and the birthplace of my joy.

Chapter 12
The last darkness of Love

Love is our capitulation. Our whole lives are governed by a longing without words on a journey with no map, to a place we do not know. Our destiny calls us to the covenant of a far horizon that is as close as the touch of our own hearts. To allow it, we must walk, naked and vulnerable, through the darkness and light of the next unknown moment.

* * *

There is one holy death in life to which we have yet to submit; a death that fills us with light. Only when we let go the safety of all we know and fall as deeply as we can into the vulnerability and nakedness of the heart, are we finally revealed as the Love to which we belong.

* * *

The sacred intimacy of Love is the only beacon that can hold us true

The last darkness of Love

through the long night of our loneliness to the dawn of a new communion.

* * *

Around us, in the living world, everything surrenders in a universal faith to a sacred will greater than itself. Everything worships Love in the temples of its cells. All Being listens and submits to the poetry of its cause.

While we dedicate our lives to pursuing happiness, it is the secret of our sorrow that breaks us free and calls us home to the ocean of Grace and Mercy that is forever flowing into our lives.

* * *

No one is left behind. No one is forgotten. Love can never let us go. Its light shines into all hearts that have been polished bright by suffering. In these moments, something accomplishes itself in us that we are not able to accomplish by ourselves…

…we are plunged into the vastness of our Source, where nothing is separate and we can never be alone. For an instant, we are shown a timeless life beyond death. These sacred moments are so often lost in the loudness of the joys and sorrows that shatter our silence.

* * *

We spend our lives trying to think our way past the inevitability of our own ending, yet we discover that we cannot confront death from a safe distance. There is no escape from the price that must be paid.

Our refusal lies in an ever-alert mind, straining to see ahead of us and make sense of what is happening. Our true path is to be still and

Love and the Sacred Song of the Hedgerow

allow the life inside us and outside us to be known, through the heart, as the tidal swell of an immortal, sacred Mercy.

Each small insurrection of letting go the mind's will is a crack through which Grace can slip to reveal the reality of Love to us.

Love brings itself to its own homecoming through a supplicant heart that is no longer led by our own will. This is the renunciation that reveals our light in the darkness.

* * *

We are willed to relinquish our separation for a union beyond our knowing that is yet to reveal itself but which, from the deep mystery of being souled, we already sense to be true.

Who amongst us is willing to give up the known for all that lies beyond; to place themselves in jeopardy? In each tender moment of faith we face the dark light of our wounding and healing, and our suffering draws to it the grace of a loving Care.

* * *

I must die to all that impedes my wisdom-journey towards the oneness of divine Love. I have to let go my "knowing what this is" and my reliance on the security of my understanding, and risk no longer defending myself against what has yet to come.

When we dare to leave behind the familiarity of all our doing and renounce all that anchors us in the safe harbour of our control, a hand reaches out to catch us: we are granted the grace of trusting that Love's Mercy will sustain and protect our passage across the wild, uncharted landscape of the next moment.

The last darkness of Love

* * *

From this time on, the precedence of the senses, the mind and the emotions gently retreat into the void of a great silence. We let them go. All must be still in order to receive the truth of who we are.

Words like consciousness, divine Love, benediction, mercy, grace and forgiveness become a new, living language that reveals us to our holiness through the prism of one last sacrifice.

Love, as the grace of its mercy, brings us to the liberation of our ego's baptism in the sacred. It waits, on the breath of an eternal patience, for the flame of our own remorse to burn brightly in the kingdom of the heart.

* * *

I have to dare to agree to be loved completely and to love completely. All my healing and all the fear and shame I overcome brings me face-to-face with this moment when I offer up all my vulnerability and hand myself over to Love.

This journey from fear and separation to joy and oneness can only take place in the resonance and solitude of my own body. This is the holy wilderness into which I have no choice but to enter naked, without food or water or the certainty of anything I hold dear.

Darkness always gives way to light. The reclusive unconsciousness of our bodies can be filled with the celestial fire of conscious Love. No one is excluded from this destiny, once the sacred courage of our heart flowers in us as the faithfulness of our own self-giving.

Love and the Sacred Song of the Hedgerow

The Light we long for is as close to us as our own skin and as distant as what we love next.

We can be led to the gateway of our heart's desire by all that we sense is true and by all the guides that have blessed our journey with their presence,- either in person or through their resounding words that echo timelessly across the centuries - yet it has to be our hand pressing at the gate, our wish and our heart that begs for entry at the door of what cannot be seen; it has to be our hand upon a key that only Love can turn.

* * *

All that we tried to defend, in defiance of the dark infinity of Loss, must now be given away as the last known act of who we were.

Anything that is to happen beyond this moment has nothing to do with the "me" that is being left behind, clinging to a hope it does not understand. From now on it is all up to Love.

* * *

The death of all that we are abandons us to a future that can no longer be lived on our terms. From now on what is accomplished accomplishes itself in us and brings us into its own perfection.

It demands the sacrifice of our own separateness for a new communion of Being with all life. Our final consent to being loved is to surrender all that we are.

Each day on my journey offers me the living knowledge that only Love can make sense of my existence. The bright fire of Love has always burned in me, yet, in the embers of my lostness, I saw only a

The last darkness of Love

life that gave way to death. Now, aflame in Love again, I know a death in me that gives way to life.

* * *

I recognise that Love finds me when I am most lost and most naked in the poverty of all that I once used to define and signify myself to be.

From the cathedral space of each one of our cells to the infinity of the cosmos, we discover in Love that our life is connected by a deathless bond to all that exists.

We return from the wilderness of our hidden path as beings of light through whom Love flows freely into a life that is now witnessed from the heart of our prayer and our praise.

* * *

Wherever we see life, we see Love giving itself away in the glory of its own sacrifice; and wherever we see death, we see Love in its tender Mercy. Love holds us to the unity of all things. We belong to the Blessing of Love, gently carrying all that exists in its invincible Care.

Our fidelity and loyalty to the infinite Love that is giving itself to us, is to face our suffering as an act of love towards ourself, in Love's name. We are beauty in search of a beholder beyond the limits of our sight and senses.

We stand revealed, in the naked holiness of our vulnerability before Love, as the majesty of a human heart, filled with the presence of divine Love - a heart that is all-knowing and all-seeing and all-loving both in all that is and as all that is. We have been discovered in the mystery of our own existence.

Love and the Sacred Song of the Hedgerow

* * *

The transmutation of our woundedness into the beauty of surrender is the destiny of us all. The penance of all that still separates us is to offer our pain to Love so that all our remaining darkness can be lit by the joyful light of perfect compassion.

In the silence of Love's dark light, the last forgiveness of our tears gently breaks us free from the power of our own past.

Love weeps itself into the shadows of our pain, yet we no longer fear it as the dread of our annihilation. Let it come! Let there be Light! Let all that has suffered in me be lit by this sacred flame so that I may step into the dark light of all that loves me through the holiness of all that was broken.

In my gratitude, I see that the hedgerow has walked with me towards this place, the silent voice of its God forever sounding its loving truth. For the last thirty years, I have laid all the days of my life at its altar and it has laughed me gently towards heaven.

* * *

We reach a door where nothing, not even our wish for the light, can be carried across its threshold. It is the parting of all that would have its will asserted. All that we have to offer now is the anguish of a separation we cannot bear.

Love is always with us, pouring its eternal Mercy upon our suffering, In the sacred presence of this Holiness there is no movement away from pain or towards pleasure. Our joy, now, is to stay.

In this stillness, Love illuminates us, celebrates our humanity, bows before our precious vulnerability and glories in the tribute of our

The last darkness of Love

willing surrender. We become our destiny. We become our own rebirth as joy, as all creation, as the unity to which all belong.

* * *

And so it comes to this. We have carried in us the priceless treasure of our suffering, all the while begging the world for its fools gold.

The sorrow of all that we have ever lost is carved upon our hearts by Love. Now, naked and alone, we are called to submit to one final parting - our own death in life and the sweeping away of the fragile shelter of all we hold dear.

This is the abyss created by the mind into which only the heart can dare to step when there is no sign of a bridge or a hand in the darkness to catch us when we fall. Only our wordless faith, born in all the echoing of home, is capable of this courage.

* * *

As we stand on the precipice of our next breath, alive in our own heart, we are divine.

Now, having sacrificed all that we are, in the first moment of our new life, the divine Sorrow that has forever watched over us carries us across all division and reveals itself as the eternity of Joy.

The rich majesty of what we have become flows back to the Source from which it came. At last! We are Home!
We are Love!

About the Author

Alastair has been a contemplative psychotherapist for the last 25 years. He blends mystical christianity, buddhism and western psychology as a way to approach psychological and spiritual healing - through an understanding of the deepest relationship between suffering, divine love and nature.

This is Alastair's second book.

He has written articles on silence and reverence in psychotherapy and, in 2010, published *The Lost Way: the call*, a fictional account of a group of contemporary spiritual seekers, being led by one of the original disciples into the deeper meaning of the beatitudes.

Alastair McNeilage ACPP, UKCP
    Contact Alastair at: awaytobetogether.com.

Printed in Great Britain
by Amazon